SEVEN VICTORIAN POETS

Edited with an Introduction and Commentary

by

DAVID WRIGHT

HEINEMANN

LONDON

Heinemann Educational Books Ltd

LONDON MELBOURNE TORONTO
SINGAPORE JOHANNESBURG AUCKLAND
IBADAN HONG KONG NAIROBI

INTRODUCTION AND COMMENTARY
© DAVID WRIGHT 1964

FIRST PUBLISHED 1964
REPRINTED 1969

SBN 435 15038 3 (cased edition)
SBN 435 15039 0 (paperback)

Published by
Heinemann Educational Books Ltd
40 Charles Street, London W1X 8AH
Printed in Great Britain by Morrison and Gibb Ltd
London and Edinburgh

SEVEN
VICTORIAN POETS

CONTENTS

ALGERNON CHARLES SWINBURNE
(1837–1909)

Choruses from *Atalanta in Calydon:*

COMMENTARY AND NOTES

Illustration to Tennyson's
The Palace of Art
by D. G. Rossetti

When Hunt, Millais and Rossetti were invited to contribute illustrations to the 1859 edition of Tennyson's *Poems*, it was a sign that Pre-Raphaelitism has 'arrived'. This drawing of Rossetti's exhibits many of the characteristics, good and bad, of Pre-Raphaelite poetry: a vague medievalism and a mood of dreamy romanticism allied to precision of imagery and attention to detail.

INTRODUCTION [1]

IT is accepted that Tennyson and Browning are the major Victorian poets. It was accepted by the Victorians, and by Tennyson and Browning. The Victorians were very conscious that theirs was a great age. Willy-nilly Tennyson, and to a less extent Browning, were made to feel self-conscious of their responsibilities. A great age demanded great poets. In listening to this demand they were not unaffected by the Victorian climate of moral earnestness that was the legacy of Thomas Arnold, the educational reformer and headmaster of Rugby. Tennyson in particular felt impelled to produce 'major' works—as it were, the official prestige-poems of the age. In so far as he surrendered to this pressure he was liable to misapply or distort his genius, as in the tinsel *Idylls of the King* (which Swinburne derisively labelled the *Morte D'Albert*) or his blank verse plays emulating Shakespeare. It is not that these works are insincere—they are full of a distressing sincerity—but that they are unreal. A clearer-headed if less great contempory of Tennyson's put his finger on the weakness of such poems as the *Idylls* when he wrote:

> I tremble for something factitious,
> Some malpractice of heart and illegitimate process;
> We are so prone to these things, with our terrible notions of duty.

The lines were written by Arthur Hugh Clough, who had been a pupil of Thomas Arnold's and sustained—or it may be cracked under—the full weight of that remarkable man's moral dynamism. All this is not to debunk Tennyson, who was a very considerable, but not in the final count a supreme poet, but to suggest that the

---

[1] Individual accounts of the lives and work of the poets in this anthology will be found in the notes at the end of the volume.

most interesting and often the clearest reflection of the Victorian period is to be found not in its eminent but in its second-string or off-beat poets, for example Clough himself.

Two reasons may be put forward. Firstly, the prime influence on Victorian poetry was the poetry of the English 'romantic revival' —Wordsworth, Keats, Shelley, and Byron (not, however, the urbane, airier, colloquial Byron of *Don Juan* and *A Vision of Judgement*, but the earlier Byron of *Childe Harold's Pilgrimage*, or of such Gothic verse-romances as *The Giaour, Lara,* and the like). The formal and artificial diction of eighteenth-century poetry was abandoned in favour of a more thrilling and exuberant language like that of the Elizabethan poetry from which it drew sustenance. Yet the Elizabethan poets took their colourful diction from the living speech of the day; while the 'romantic revivalists' and the Victorians in general drew theirs from their reading of Elizabethan poetry. However, to a greater or less degree, some of the minor Victorian poets—for instance Clough, Patmore, Barnes, and to some extent Christina Rossetti, kept alive the vocabulary, syntax, and inflection of ordinary speech in their verse —at least, more of it is present in their work than in the bulk of Victorian poetry.

Secondly, it is those lesser Victorian poets who did not feel themselves bound to speak for the age—or rather, to provide it with its status-poems—who directly reflected its uneasiness. The Victorian era was superficially placid. After 1815 England was involved in no major war for a century; 1848, the year of revolutions that shook kings from their thrones like so many acorns, passed England by. The age was marked by scientific progress, industrial and imperial expansion, growing prosperity and smugness. But at heart it was agitated by doubt and even horror. All seemed solid; yet the basis of social order had cracked under the impact of the French Revolution of 1789. The concept, bequeathed by the Age of Reason, of the universe as a logical clockwork mechanism was disappearing. It had been proved that Man was created before 4004 BC. The literal truth of the Bible might no longer be taken for granted. In consequence some, like John Henry Newman, were inclined to take refuge in the authority of the Church, which finally led him and others of the Tractarian, or Oxford Movement, to the dogma of Roman Catholicism. Some, like Clough, became rudderless, lost their faith and turned agnostic; some, like Matthew Arnold, substituted morality for God. In reading the minor poetry of the time one detects an awareness that a new and horrifying world was being born. This can be seen in the haunted, sometimes nightmarish, productions of early nineteenth-century poets like George Darley, Thomas Hood, and T. L. Beddoes —the titles of such poems as *The Last Man* and *Death's Jest Book* indicate the themes that obsessed them—as well as in later poets like Edward Lear whose melancholy nonsense-verses are an allegory of human solitude and despair; in poems like Alexander Smith's *Glasgow;* and especially in the work of James Thomson ('B.V.') whose *City of Dreadful Night* is in some ways the most powerful long poem of the Victorian age—reminiscent, even, of *The Waste Land. The City of Dreadful Night* can be seen as a symbolic and apocalyptic vision of the world brought into being by the Industrial Revolution at the end of the eighteenth century. Mass-production was making possible the mass-populations of the new industrial towns. And mass-populations meant the breaking-down of traditional social organization; the organic society of small towns where everybody knew his neighbour was being replaced by vast anonymous agglomerations.

> Yes, here and there some weary wanderer
>   In that same city of tremendous night,
> Will understand a speech, and feel a stir
>   Of fellowship in all-disastrous fight;
> 'I suffer mute and lonely, yet another
> Uplifts his voice to let me know a brother
>   Travels the same wild paths though out of sight.'

Factory workers were herded together in appalling congeries in which human beings lost individuality; a new creature, whom the Spanish philosopher Ortega y Gasset has called the Mass-man, was just beginning to emerge. This in turn was to result in a levelling process, in the premium placed on ordinariness and mediocrity, and the down-grading of whatever was individual, personal, and uniquely excellent. Thomas Carlyle, the home-made philosopher, historian, and visionary, sensed this and uttered his Cassandra warnings and admonishments against the mob in such books as *On Heroes and Hero-Worship*. So, too, in urbaner style, did Clough's friend Matthew Arnold in his literary criticism.

Clough and Arnold are in many ways the central poets of the Victorian period. In their parallel though differing reactions to nineteenth-century 'philistinism' and the mass-values imposed by the industral revolution, they are the nearest English equivalent to Baudelaire. Clough may have been in his life and work 'a foil'd circuitous wanderer', but his best poetry questions the assumptions of his time with an ironic detachment and a clear-sighted, un-sentimental intelligence that make it peculiarly modern in tone compared with the elegiac melancholy of Arnold. This can best be seen in his two long poems, *The Bothie of Tober-na-Vuolich* and particularly *Amours de Voyage*, which should be read whole (and they are surprisingly gay and readable) as their effect is cumulative and does not lend itself easily to extracts; or in the ironic adhortations—some are included in this anthology—of the Spirit in *Dipsychus*. A brilliant future had been predicted for Clough when he was at Oxford; but when he died at the age of forty-two in 1861 he was regarded by his friends as a failure. Yet it could also be said that Arnold, who elegized him in *Thyrsis*, never fulfilled himself as a poet; after 1867, when he was forty-five, Arnold scarcely wrote another line but devoted himself to critical writing on literary, social, and religious themes.

Arnold's poetry is far more even and formally accomplished than Clough's, but—except for *Dover Beach*—belongs more earnestly to its time. There is a dichotomy in Arnold's poetry, because he never clearly recognized the sort of poet he was. In his criticism he inveighed against the errors of the 'romantic revival' in English poetry—the school of Keats and Shelley—yet in diction and

4

sensibility his poems owe everything to it. And Arnold really belonged, whether he knew it or not, to that larger Romantic Movement of the nineteenth century in Europe. This came into being when the effects of the Industrial Revolution began to manifest themselves; it questioned the validity of the assumptions of material progress, and was fundamentally a reaction of intelligent and sensitive minds (De Maistre, Stendhal, Delacroix, Kierkegaard, and Baudelaire were of their number, as well as Heine, whom Arnold championed and helped to introduce to the English public) against the levelling tendencies of mass-democracy, the inflation of the mediocre, and increasing devaluation of the individual and unique. Hence Arnold's doctrine of an intellectual *élite* and sustained attack on 'philistinism' (i.e. the materialism of the new middle classes; the word is borrowed from Heine) which is the ground-bass of his literary and social criticism. Hence too his solitary Scholar Gipsies fleeing from 'the world's heart-wearying roar'. The Scholar Gipsy, who turned his back on society and its rewards to pursue his vision, is Arnold's symbol for the poet in an age of middle-class values and mores. It is no accident that the Scholar Gipsy makes a ghostly reappearance in Arnold's elegy for Clough. Though Clough never quite succeeded in coming to terms with society till the last, poetically barren years of his life, neither he nor Arnold decisively turned their backs upon it as did Baudelaire, their saturnine contemporary across the Channel.

In the two fine Oxford elegies and in *Stanzas from the Grande Chartreuse* the tone of Arnold's protest is puzzled and melancholy —plaintive and somehow not quite real. Arnold was too indoctrinated with his father's muscular puritanism wholly to disbelieve, like Baudelaire, in the idea of progress—that universal nineteenth-century panacea for all evil. (The waning of religious belief in the light of scientific discoveries was largely compensated for by the theory of human progress.) This is one reason why, in spite of his urbanity, intellectualism, and receptivity to European currents of thought, so many of Arnold's poems remain provincially Victorian. There is a grand exception, *Dover Beach*; and only

5

here, where 'the sea of faith' is seen receding from 'the naked shingles of the world' which

> Hath really neither joy, nor love, nor light,
> Nor certitude, nor peace, nor help for pain;

from its 'darkling plain'

> Swept with confused alarms of struggle and flight,
> Where ignorant armies clash by night

is Arnold's real pessimism squarely presented. It is more nakedly pessimistic than anything in Baudelaire. Unlike Baudelaire, Arnold believed in morality and uplift rather than God. Thus it was, as T. S. Eliot says, 'literature, or Culture, tended with Arnold to usurp the place of Religion.' 'The end is everywhere,' as Arnold makes Goethe say in *Memorial Verses*: 'Art still has truth; take refuge there!' And this, precisely, is what the Pre-Raphaelites, D. G. Rossetti and his friends, who shaded off with Swinburne into the Aesthetic Movement ('art for art's sake') and the decadent poets of the *fin-de-siècle* (such as Ernest Dowson and Lionel Johnson) were to do.

But before discussing the Pre-Raphaelites a word must be said about Coventry Patmore and William Barnes. Patmore is sometimes regarded as a Pre-Raphaelite. It is true the Pre-Raphaelites admired his poetry and imagined it to be in tune with their aesthetic notions; Patmore, however, never thought of himself as one of them. Nor did he think highly of Rossetti's verse (he preferred the early Tennyson). Patmore was an enigma and a paradox. A Roman Catholic convert, he was violently anti-clerical. His poem *The Angel in the House* won him the title of 'laureate of marriage', nonetheless he had three wives. His independence of mind was extreme to the point of eccentricity. Patmore developed into a kind of patriarchal aristocrat and has usually been regarded as a typical Victorian, yet it was he, rather than such self-consciously Bohemian or *avant-garde* figures as Rossetti and Swinburne, who really swam against the current of the age. He saw through the cant of sentimental

Victorian liberalism, its peculiarly stultifying prudery and puritanism, its faith in progress and human perfectibility (which he once called 'the most infallible sign of a feeble intellect').

There is no general agreement about the place of Patmore in nineteenth-century poetry. Some critics have put it very high indeed. On one hand he has been compared with the metaphysical poets of the seventeenth century—his verse shows something of that sort of wit—and even with Dante; on the other he has been laughed at as a Victorian sentimentalist. His long poem *The Angel in the House* was so enormously popular in his time that the tendency since then has been to underrate it. His last poetical work—*The Unknown Eros,* a collection of interrelated odes using a new metrical technique—was ignored when it first appeared and has been given comparatively little attention since. Yet *The Angel in the House* is eminently readable. No other poet apart from Chaucer has attempted its subject: by taking marriage as the theme of his *magnum opus* Patmore at least showed originality. In giving his poem a realistic contemporary setting and maintaining a gaiety of tone and what may be called a formally colloquial style, Patmore matched Clough's achievement in *Amours de Voyage.*

Patmore's dedication to poetry was absolute: he believed in the sacred character of the poetic vocation. Towards the end of his life he formed a friendship with Gerard Manley Hopkins, whose poetry was so far in advance of its time that it was not to be published until 1918. Hopkins admired Patmore's poetry; and though Patmore, then an old man, could not understand or like Hopkins' experiments, he had enormous respect for Hopkins' critical judgement and submitted to it (as the published correspondence of the two men shows) with surprising humility. It is worth noting that Hopkins and Patmore were the only two Victorian poets who contributed anything of real value to the theory of English prosody[1]; some of Hopkins' ideas may have been a development of Patmore's. And both Hopkins and Patmore shared a high opinion of the little-regarded regional poet, William Barnes. It was the poetic integrity

[1] See Notes, p. 165.

of Barnes, alone of all the Victorian poets, that Patmore whole-heartedly admired.

Barnes' niche in English poetry is still unrecognized, though he is not forgotten. His poetry is much nearer to the moderns than has been suspected. It belongs to that underground stream of Victorian poetry in which the prosody of modern English verse is rooted; it influenced both Thomas Hardy and G. M. Hopkins. Barnes' real position in English poetry has been obscured not so much by the fact that half his verse was written in the Dorset dialect as by his label, 'The Dorset Poet' which is true enough but thoroughly misleading. Although it is a fact that his poetry is almost entirely confined to Dorset subjects, he was a metrical innovator and experimentalist as well as one of the few nineteenth-century poets who consistently put into practice Wordsworth's injunction in the *Preface to Lyrical Ballads* to employ in poetry 'the language really used by men'. Barnes began writing poems in the Dorset dialect in his early thirties. But at least half his poems are written in common English. And, unlike Robert Burns, he achieved poetry of as high an order in standard English as he did in his dialect verse. Though he called the Dorset dialect his 'native tongue' he did not speak it himself by way of ordinary conversation. Barnes employed dialect to detach himself from the artificial 'poetical' and literary language that was the bane of nineteenth-century poetry. He wrote about a traditional rural way of life that was fast disappearing and already archaic; yet his verse does not date like so much Victorian poetry. This is not because Barnes confined himself to the pastoral—he wrote valid poems about bicycles and railway trains, subjects that defeated many Victorian poets—it is because he was able to avoid a 'literary' language. Thus he escaped the weakness of most nineteenth-century poetry: a vocabulary and mode of expression that derives from the written rather than the spoken word. Like the giant Antaeus whose strength diminished when he lost contact with his mother earth, poetry becomes debilitated when it loses touch with the forms and usages of the spoken word. Barnes kept that contact; it was a valuable service. He may not have been a poet in the class of Robert Burns or John Clare; his scope was too limited, even if deliberately limited. He refused to treat the less pleasant aspects of the human condition. His poems may have been no more than quiet elegies for pre-Industrial England; but he was a master craftsman and deserved Coventry Patmore's verdict, 'He has done a small thing well while his contemporaries have mostly been engaged in doing big things ill'.

And this, perhaps, was the trouble with the Pre-Raphaelites. The comment of Ford Madox Ford, writing in 1911, just before Pound and Eliot began the revolution in poetry, is still true:

> They took themselves with such extreme seriousness—these Pre-Raphaelite poets—and nevertheless I have always fancied that they are responsible for the death of English poetry. My father once wrote of Rossetti that he put down the thoughts of Dante in the language of Shakespeare, and the words seem to me to be extremely true and extremely damning. For what is wanted of a poet is that he should express his own thoughts in the language of his own time. This, with perhaps the solitary exception of Christina Rossetti, the Pre-Raphaelite poets never thought of.

To begin with, the original Pre-Raphaelite Brotherhood was an association of young painters—D. G. Rossetti, Millais, and Holman Hunt—united in a revolt against the academic art-fashions of the day and in an attempt to revitalize art by a return to the simplicity of medieval painting. Their ideas derived partly from Ruskin's *Modern Painters*, wherein Raphael is condemned because he was the first painter to replace the unvarnished depiction of actualities by a stylish convention. Fidelity to nature was their battlecry; Sir Joshua Reynolds their *bête noir*; and they championed the then little-known works of Keats and Blake. The group brought out a short-lived magazine, *The Germ*—the original ancestor of the 'little reviews' which were to exercise so much influence on writing in the first decades of the twentieth century. As a definite association the Pre-Raphaelite Brotherhood did not survive more than a few years; but the term 'Pre-Raphaelite' came to be loosely applied to cover a kind of vague medievalism and aestheticism common to the work of later friends of Rossetti—e.g. William Morris and Swinburne.

The most typical Pre-Raphaelite poet is, of course, Rossetti himself. Superficially a rebel, and seemingly a *poète maudit*, he was more in accord with the *petit-bourgeois* sentimentalism and prudery of the Victorian age than his reputation as a bohemian and sensualist would lead one to expect. He was as much a painter as a poet; and his importance resides in the magnetism of his personality and the influence he exercised over the painters and poets of his period far more than in his actual achievement. It can be said that his most famous poems are as a general rule his worst. *The Blessed Damozel* is a case in point. It could be called the brand-image of Pre-Raphaelite poetry: a decoratively medieval setting plus a luscious plangency of rhythm are its chief ingredients, and they camouflage a mawkishness at the centre. (E.g. we are invited to contemplate the emotions of a soul in bliss languishing for an earthly lover—an impossible, not to say blasphemous, situation by the canons of medieval theology.) Rossetti's medievalism, and Pre-Raphaelite medievalism in general, owes more to the imagery of Keats' poems—particularly *The Eve of St Agnes*—than to any serious understanding of medieval thinking, literature, or art. His major poetic effort, *The House of Life*, is a rambling collection of sonnets interspersed with a number of more effective lyrics. They are intended to form a commentary on such vague but reverberating subjects as Love and Death and Change, but remain, generally speaking, a rather tumid reflection of Rossetti's emotional states of mind during his love affairs with Elizabeth Siddall and Jane Morris. In his well-known poem, *Jenny*, the subject—a prostitute—shocked Victorian prurience, yet the attitude expressed towards the girl is quite in accord with sentimental Victorian morality. It is in those lines that set a mood, like the passage describing a London dawn, that reality breaks in. For Rossetti is not a negligible poet when he has his eye on the object. Though so many of his poems are spoiled by their unreality and affectation of archaic language he could and did write plain, unadorned lyrics of great restraint and effectiveness. *My Sister's Sleep* is one whose strength lies in its quietness and fidelity of visual detail—small things precisely observed—a quality one finds in the better Pre-Raphaelite paintings. And something of the nightmare that lay close to the surface of the nineteenth century appears in his strange fragment, *The Orchard-Pit*, all that remains of a long poem he never completed.

The Pre-Raphaelites' reaction to the grim face presented by the nineteenth century was to turn their imagination away from it and inhabit a dream-world. This might be said of Rossetti's sister Christina; but the difference between her and the Pre-Raphaelites is that her dream-world is an image or reflection of reality, not a substitute or an escape from it. To understand this it is only necessary to compare the vague, shifting symbology of Rossetti's dreamier poems like *Love's Nocturn* with the precise analogies that Christina presents in such apparently fanciful poems as *The Prince's Progress* and *Goblin Market*, which are in fact moral fables. The latter, it has been pointed out, can even be read as an allegorical presentation of the fall and redemption of man. Where Rossetti suggests, Christina defines. She has feeling; Rossetti has feelings. With the exception of Emily Brontë, Christina Rossetti is easily the best of the Victorian women poets. She was not as well-read—'cultured' might be the word—as Elizabeth Barrett Browning, but her intellectual gifts were greater and considerably more disciplined. The discipline may have been the effect of her Anglican pietism. At any rate her best work has a stimulating absence of that plushy sentimentality and emotional fatuity which mars so much Victorian poetry. Like her intellect her diction is athletic and spare. She had psychological insight and a sense of humour that often comes out quite delightfully, as in *The Queen of Hearts*. The only quality that Christina Rossetti really shares with the Pre-Raphaelites is the visual precision of her imagery. She does not labour after decorative effects, and her language, unlike theirs, is fundamentally the language of ordinary speech. And it may be claimed that Christina was a pioneer: *Goblin Market* is probably the first English poem in rhymed free verse.

The poetry of Swinburne, the last poet in this anthology, is not nowadays greatly regarded and seems unlikely ever to regain the glamour it had for his contemporaries. Thomas Hardy uses an odd image to describe its impact upon Swinburne's generation:

> It was as though a garland of red roses
> Had fallen about the hood of some smug nun
> When irresponsibly dropped as from the sun,
> In fulth of numbers freaked with musical closes,
> Upon Victoria's formal middle time,
> His leaves of rhythm and rhyme.

Swinburne's technical dexterity, or 'fulth of numbers' is indeed phenomenal, but often seems a sterile dexterity, like a juggler's; almost an end in itself. Swinburne's poems are not so much poems as pieces of music in which the words serve for musical notes and do not really relate to the objects or concepts they are supposed to identify. T. S. Eliot has remarked that his poems seem to make tremendous statements, yet their meaning 'is merely the hallucination of meaning'. But one cannot dismiss Swinburne. As Coleridge said, 'the sense of musical delight, with the power of producing it, is a gift of the imagination'—a gift without which poetry cannot be made, though application may supply its other components: range, imagery, precision, and so on. Most of these are lacking in Swinburne, but not the all-important gift of music. In this sense the best of what he wrote is pure poetry—a verbal music; a poetry that stands in much the same relation to other poetry as abstract to figurative painting. Though Swinburne's verbal music is new to English verse its rhythms are by no means subtle and are often handled mechanically. Nevertheless they can still be dazzling, as in the choruses of *Atalanta in Calydon*. A remark made by one of the characters in his novel *Lesbia Brandon* is an apt summing-up of Swinburne's kind of poetry:

You can't expect one to sing sense extempore: not better sense than that. Just look down there at the sea now. There's no sense in that noise, and by Jove, is there anything like it?

There isn't anything like it; except in Swinburne.

In Swinburne's poetry there are two themes. The first is a sense of tragedy, and of the unreasoning hostile cruelty of whatever orders the world, 'the supreme evil, God'—a line that Christina Rossetti felt bound to paste over in her copy of *Atalanta*. The second is an exploitation of perversion and of the idea of the sadistic nature of love: this can be found in poems like *Anactoria* or *Dolores*, 'our Lady of Pain'. These poems are sensational rather than sensual, and they shocked Swinburne's Victorian contemporaries as they were meant to. They are not, as in Baudelaire's *Fleurs du Mal*, a true exploration of the nature of evil, but rather propaganda for a pathological state. Today Baudelaire's poems remain disturbing; Swinburne's appear slightly comic:

> Thou wert fair in the fearless old fashion,
> And thy limbs are as melodies yet,
> And move to the music of passion
> With lithe and lascivious regret.
> What ailed us, O gods, to desert you
> For creeds that refuse and restrain?
> Come down and redeem us from virtue,
> Our Lady of Pain.

Swinburne was the last of the Pre-Raphaelites. Like Rossetti's, his poetry exists in its own world, but one even more absolutely sealed off from reality. It is an aesthetic never-never land, filled with semi-medieval or classical furniture, knights in armour, nymphs and satyrs, where the climate is uniformly melodramatic.[1] Even the political and libertarian poems he wrote for the Italian revolutionary Mazzini in *Songs Before Sunrise*, belongs to it. His

[1] Thunder, lightning, rain, and full gales. One is reminded of George VI's famous remark to John Piper when he saw his series of paintings of Windsor Castle: 'By Jove, you were unlucky with the weather!'

poetry is the logical conclusion, and at its worst the *reductio ad absurdum*, of the pseudo-Elizabethan exuberance of Keats and Shelley. It is the end of a road. And that is something. After Swinburne a new direction had to be found for English poetry. Swinburne is the last eminent Victorian poet: with his work Victorian poetry reaches its terminus—a vast, windy, rococo Crystal Palace, exotic and a little silly, but not by any means negligible.

WILLIAM BARNES

Benighted

Invited by your sire's good will
   To me, I took the road
By Downley, over heath and hill,
   To go to your abode;
And o'er my mare, as white as snow,
   Full fain I sprightly threw
My leg, and in my stirrup's bow
   I set my shining shoe,
And merry-hearted,
Briskly started   10
   Out by our old yew.

But when, at last, the sun had set
   Upon my road, too soon,
I found myself where three ways met
   Below the western moon.
There stood a shining holly tree,
   With firs of five-fold height,
But yet no guide-post held for me
   An arm to set me right,
As I benighted,   20
Moon-belighted,
   Turn'd my wheeling sight.

And one road down a ground-slope sank,
  A darken'd hollow way;
And one beside a heathy bank
  Ran on as light as day;
And nigh it wound a shining brook
  Adown a shallow bed,
And thitherward my mare would look
  With ever-steadfast head,   30
As if well-knowing,
Without showing,
  Whitherward I sped.

And shortly, from the eastern sky,
  I found five bell-sounds sweep;
Your peal of bells—one shrill, one high,
  One loud, one low, one deep—
And with my moonshade on before
  My mare's two ears' white tips,
I soon had reach'd your gate, your door,   40
  Your fire of blazing chips,
Where I, at meeting,
Found a greeting,
  Out of many lips.

I never after that mistook
  The right road of the three,
And well I knew the shallow brook
  And firs, and holly tree;
I ne'er mistook the road when day
  Show'd houses from afar,
Nor when the moon was o'er my way,
  Nor by the evening star,
As I rode spanking
On by banking,
  Gapp'd for gate or bar.

Troubles of the Day

As there, along the elmy hedge, I go
   By banksides white with parsley—parsley-bloom—
Where smell of new-mown hay comes wafted by
   On wind of dewy evening, evening gloom,
And homeward take my shaded way between
The hedge's high-tipp'd wood, and barley green,
     I sing, or mean
'O troubles of the day. Flee to the west,
Come not my homeward way. I seek my rest.'

The dairy cows, by meadow trees, lie free   10
   Of calls to milker's pails—the milkmaids' calls;
The horses now have left their rolling wheels
   And reel'd in home to stable, to their stalls,
And down the grey-pool'd stream the fish awhile
Are free from all the prowling angler's guile,
     And o'er the stile
I sink, and sing or say, 'Flee to the west
O troubles of the day. I seek my rest.'

My boy—whose little, high-rigg'd boat, athwart
   The windy pool, by day, at afternoon,   20
Has fluttered, tippling like a bird
   That tries to fly unfledged, to fly too soon—
Now sleeps forgetful of the boat, and fond
Old dog that he had taught to swim the pond.
     So flee beyond
The edge of sinking day, towards the west,
Ye troubles flee away. I seek my rest.

A star is o'er the tower on the hill,
    Whence rings no clanging knell, no evening peal;
The mill stands dark beside the flouncing foam;   30
    But still is all its gear, its mossy wheel.
No rooks now sweep along the darkened sky,
And o'er the road few feet or wheels go by.
        So fly, O fly
Ye troubles, with the day, adown the west,
Come not along my way. I seek my rest.

Be'mi'ster

Sweet Be'mi'ster, that bist a-bound [1]
By green and woody hills all round,
Wi' hedges, reachèn [2] up between
A thousan' vields o' zummer green,
Where elems' lofty heads do drow [3]
Their sheädes vor haÿ-meakers below,
An' wild hedge-flow'rs do charm the souls
O' maïdens in their evenèn strolls

When I o' Zunday nights wi' Jeäne
Do saunter drough [4] a vield or leäne,   10
Where elder-blossoms be a-spread
Above the eltrot's [5] milk-white head,
An' flow'rs o' blackberries do blow
Upon the brembles, white as snow,
To be outdone avore my zight
By Jeäne's gay frock o' dazzlèn white;

[1] is bounded   [2] reaching   [3] throw   [4] through   [5] cow-parsley

Oh! then there's nothèn that's 'ithout
Thy hills that I do ho about,[1]—
Noo bigger pleäce, noo gaÿer town,
Beyond thy sweet bells' dyèn soun',   20
As they do ring, or strike the hour,
At evenèn vrom thy wold [2] red tow'r.
No: shelter still my head, an' keep
My bwones when I do vall asleep.

The Bwoat

Where cows did slowly seek the brink
O' Stour, drough zunburnt grass, to drink;
Wi' vishèn [3] float, that there did sink
    An' rise, I zot [4] as in a dream.
The dazzlèn sun did cast his light
On hedge-row blossom, snowy white,
Though nothèn yet did come in zight,
    A-stirrèn on the straÿèn stream;

Till, out by sheädy [5] rocks there show'd
A bwoat along his foamy road,   10
Wi' thik feaïr maïd [6] at mill, a-row'd
    Wi' Jeane behind her brother's oars.
An' steätely as a queen o' vo'k [7]
She zot [8] wi' floatèn scarlet cloak,
An' comèn on, at ev'ry stroke,
    Between my withy-sheäded shores.

---

[1] long for   [2] old   [3] fishing   [4] sat   [5] shady   [6] this fair maid   [7] folk   [8]sat

The broken stream did idly try
To show her sheäpe a-ridèn by,
The rushes brown-bloomed stems did ply,
    As if they bow'd to her by will.   20
The rings o' water, wi' a sock,[1]
Did break upon the mossy rock,
An' gi'e my beatèn heart a shock,
    Above my float's up-leapèn quill.

Then, lik' a cloud below the skies,
A-drifted off, wi' less'nèn size,
An' lost, she floated vrom my eyes,
    Where down below the stream did wind;
An' left the quiet weäves woonce mwore [2]
To zink at rest, a sky-blue'd vloor,[3]   30
Wi' all so still's the clote [4] they bore
    Aye, all but my own ruffled mind.

The Wold Wall

Here, Jeäne, we vu'st [5] did meet below
The leafy boughs, a-swingèn slow,
Avore [6] the zun, wi' evenèn glow,
    Above our road, a-beamèn red;
The grass in zwath [7] wer in the meäds,
The water gleam'd among the reeds
In aïr a-steälèn roun' the hall,
Where ivy clung upon the wall.
Ah! well-a-day! O wall adieu!
The wall is wold, my grief is new.   10

[1] *sobbing noise*   [2] *waves once more*   [3] *floor*   [4] *waterlily*   [5] *first*   [6] *before*
[7] *in swath*, i.e., *mown*

An' there you walk'd wi' blushèn pride,
Where softly-wheelèn streams did glide.
Drough sheädes o' poplars at my zide,
An' there wi' love that still do live,
Your feäce did wear the smile o' youth,
The while you spoke wi' age's truth,
An' wi' a rwosebud's mossy ball,
I deck'd your bosom vrom the wall.
Ah! well-a-day! O wall adieu!
The wall is wold, my grief is new.   20

But now when winter's raïn do vall,
An' wind do beät ageän the hall,
The while upon the wat'ry wall
In spots o' grey the moss do grow;
The ruf ¹ noo mwore shall overspread
The pillor ² ov our weary head,
Nor shall the rose's mossy ball
Behang vor you the house's wall.
Ah! well-a-day! O wall adieu!
The wall is wold, my grief is new.   30

When Birds be Still

Vor all the zun do leäve the sky,
An' all the zounds o' day do die,
An' noo mwore veet ³ do walk the dim
Vield-path to clim' the stiël's bars,
Yeet ⁴ out below the rizèn stars,
The dark'nèn day mid leäve behind
Woone ⁵ tongue that I shall always vind,
A-whisperèn kind, when birds be still.

¹ *roof*   ² *pillow*   ³ *feet*   ⁴ *Yet*   ⁵ *One*

Zoo let the day come on to spread
His kindly light above my head
Wi' zights to zee, an' sounds to hear,
That still do cheer my thoughtvul mind;
Or let en goo, an' leäve behind
An hour to stroll along the gleädes,
Where night do drown the beeches' sheädes,
On grasses' bleädes, when birds be still.

Vor when the night do lull the sound
O' cows a-bleärèn out in ground,[1]
The sh'ill-vaïced [2] dog do stan' an' bark
'Ithin the dark, bezide the road;
An' when noo cracklèn waggon's lwoad
Is in the leäne, the wind do bring
The merry peals that bells do ring
O ding-dong-ding, when birds be still.

Zoo teäke, vor me, the town a-drown'd,
'Ithin a storm o' rumblèn sound,
An' gi'e me vaïces that do speak
So soft an' meek, to souls alwone;
The brook a-gurglèn round a stwone,
An' birds o' day a-zingèn clear
An' leaves, that I mid zit an' hear
A-rustlèn near, when birds be still.

10

20

30

[1] *out in the fields*   [2] *shrill-voiced*

Lydlinch Bells

When skies wer peäle wi' twinklèn stars,
An' whislèn aïr a-risèn keen;
An' birds did leäve the icy bars
To vind, in woods, their mossy screen;
When vrozen grass, so white's a sheet,
Did scrunchy sharp below our veet,
An' water, that did sparkle red
At zunzet, wer a-vrozen dead;
The ringers then did spend an hour
A-ringèn changes up in tow'r;   10
Vor Lydlinch bells be good vor sound,
An' liked by all the naïghbours round.

An' while along the leafless boughs
O' ruslèn hedges, win's ¹ did pass,
An' orts ² ov haÿ, a-left by cows,
Did russle on the vrozen grass,
An' maïdens' païls, wi' all their work
A-done, did hang upon their vurk,³
An' they, avore the fleämèn ⁴ brand,
Did teäke their needle-work in hand,   20
The men did cheer their heart an hour
A ringèn changes up in tow'r;
Vor Lydlinch bells be good vor sound,
An' lik'd by all the naïghbours round.

¹ *winds*   ² *remnants*   ³ *fork (of a pail-stand)*   ⁴ *flaming*

23

There sons did pull the bells that rung
Their mothers' weddèn peals avore,
The while their fathers led em young
An' blushèn vrom the churches door,
An' still did cheem, wi' happy sound
As time did bring the Zundays round,　　　　　30
An' call em to the holy pleäce
Vor heavenly gifts o' peace an' greäce;
An' vo'k did come, a-streamèn slow
Along below the trees in row,
While they, in merry peals, did sound
The bells vor all the naïghbours round.

An' when the bells, wi' changèn peal,
Did smite their own vo'ks window-peänes,
Their sof'en'd sound did often steal
Wi' west winds drough the Bagber leänes;　　　40
Or, as the win' did shift, mid goo [1]
Where woody Stock do nessle lew,[2]
Or where the risèn moon did light
The walls o' Thornhill on the height;
An' zoo, whatever time mid bring
To meäke their vive clear vaices zing,
Still Lydlinch bells wer good vor sound
An' liked by all the naïghbours round.

[1] *even went*　　[2] *nestles in shelter*

Shaftesbury Feäir

When hillborne Paladore did show
So bright to me down miles below
As woonce the zun, a-rollèn west,
Did brighten up his hill's high breast
Wi' walls a-lookèn dazzlèn white,
Or yollow, on the grey-topp'd height
Of Paladore, as peäle day wore
    Awaÿ so feäir.
Oh! how I wish'd that I wer there.

The pleäce wer too vur off to spy   10
The livèn vo'k a-passèn by;
The vo'k too vur vor aïr [1] to bring
The words that they did speak or zing.
All dum' to me wer each abode,
An' empty wer the down-hill road
Vrom Paladore, as peäle day wore
    Awaÿ so feäir;
But how I wish'd that I wer there.

But when I clomb the lofty ground
Where livèn veet an' tongues did sound,   20
At feäir,[2] bezide your bloomèn feäce,
The pertiest [3] in all the pleäce,
As you did look, wi' eyes as blue
As yonder southern hills in view,
Vrom Paladore—O Polly dear,
    Wi' you up there,
How merry then wer I at feäir.

[1] *too far for air*   [2] *At the fair*   [3] *prettiest*

Since vu'st I trod thik steep hill-zide
My grievèn soul'v a-been a-tried
Wi' pain, an' loss o' worldly geär,
An souls a-gone I wanted near;
But you be here too goo up still,
An' look to Blackmwore vrom the hill
O' Paladore. Zoo, Polly dear,
     We'll goo up there,
An' spend an hour or two at feäir.

The wold brown meäre's a-brought vrom grass,
An' rubb'd an' cwombed so bright as glass;
An' now we'll hitch her in, an' start
To feäir upon the new green cart,
An' teäke our little Poll between
Our zides, as proud's a little queen,
To Paladore. Aye, Poll a dear,
     Vor now 'tis feäir,
An' she's a-longèn to goo there.

While Paladore, on watch, do straïn
Her eyes to Blackmwore's blue-hilled pläin,
While Duncliffe is the traveller's mark,
Or cloty [1] Stour's a-rollèn dark;
Or while our bells do call, vor greäce,
The vo'k avore their Seävior's [2] feäce,
Mid [3] Paladore, an' Poll a dear,
     Vor ever know
O' peäce an' plenty down below.

         [1] *water-lilied*   [2] *Saviour's*   [3] *May*

30

40

50

Eclogue :
John, Jealous at Shroton Feäir

Jeäne; her Brother; John, her Sweetheart; and Racketèn Joe.

JEÄNE

I'm thankvul I be out o' that
Thick crowd, an' not asquot [1] quite flat.
'That ever we should plunge in where the vo'k do drunge [2]
So tight's the cheese-wring on the veät!
I've scarce a thing a-left in pleäce.
'Tis all a-tore vrom pin an' leäce.
My bonnet's like a wad, a-beat up to a dod,
An' all my heäir's about my feäce.

HER BROTHER

Here come an' zit out here a bit,
An' put yourzelf to rights.   10

JOHN

No, Jeäne, no, no! Now you don't show
The very wo'st o' plights.

HER BROTHER

Come, come, there's little harm a-done;
Your hoops be out so roun's the zun.

JOHN

An' there's your bonnet back in sheäpe.

HER BROTHER

An' there's your pin, and there's your ceäpe.[3]

---

[1] *squashed*   [2] *push*   [3] *cape*

JOHN

An' there your curls do match, an' there
'S the vittiest [1] maid in all the feäir.

JEÄNE

Now look, an' tell us who's a-spied
Vrom Sturminster, or Manston zide.

HER BROTHER

There's rantèn Joe: How he do stalk,
An' zwang his whip, an' laugh, an' talk!

JOHN

An' how his head do wag, avore his steppèn lag. [2]
Jist like a pigeon's in a walk!

HER BROTHER

Heigh! there, then, Joey, ben't we proud!

JEÄNE

He can't hear you among the crowd.

HER BROTHER

Why, no the thunder peals do drown the sound o' wheels.
His own pipe is a-pitched too loud.
What, you here too?

RACKETÈN JOE

Yes, Sir, to you. 30

All o' me that's a-left.

JEÄNE

A body plump's a goodish lump
Where reämes [3] ha' such a heft. [4]

[1] *smartest* [2] *striding leg* [3] *skeletons* [4] *weight*
28

JOHN

Who lost his crown a-racèn?

RACKETÈN JOE

Who?

Zome silly chap a-backèn you.
Well, now, an' how do vo'k treat Jeäne?

JEÄNE

Why not wi' feärèns.[1]

RACKETÈN JOE

What d'ye mean,

When I've a-brought ye such a bunch
O' theäse nice ginger-nuts to crunch?   40
An' here, John, here! you teäke a vew.[2]

JOHN

No, keep em all vor Jeäne an' you!

RACKETÈN JOE

Well, Jeäne, an' when d'ye meän to come
An' call on me, then, up at hwome.
You han't a-come athirt,[3] since I'd my foot a-hurt,
A-slippèn vrom the tree I clomb.

JEÄNE

Well, if so be that you be stout
On voot ageän, you'll vind me out.

JOHN

Aye, better chaps woont goo, not many steps vor you,
If you do hawk yourzelf about.   50

[1] *fairings*   [2] *take a few*   [3] *athwart*, i.e., *near*

29

Wull John come too?

JOHN

No, thanks to you.
Two's company, dree's none.

HER BROTHER
There, don't be stung by his mad tongue,
'Tis nothèn else but fun.

JEÄNE
There, what d'ye think o' my new ceäpe?

JOHN
Why, think that 'tis an ugly sheäpe.

JEÄNE
Then you should buy me, now theäse feäir,
A mwore becomen woone to wear.

JOHN
I buy your ceäpe! No; Joe will screäpe   60
Up dibs enough to buy your ceäpe,
As things do look, to meäke you fine
Is long Joe's business mwore than mine.

JEÄNE
Lauk, John, the mwore that you do pout
The mwore he'll glene.[1]

JOHN

A yelpèn lout.

[1] *sneer*

ARTHUR HUGH CLOUGH

The Shadow

I dreamed a dream: I dreamt that I espied,
Upon a stone that was not rolled aside,
A Shadow sit upon a grave—a Shade,
As thin, as unsubstantial, as of old
Came, the Greek poet told,
To lick the life-blood in the trench Ulysses made—
As pale, as thin, and said:
'I am the Resurrection of the Dead.
The night is past, the morning is at hand,
And I must in my proper semblance stand,   10
Appear brief space and vanish,—listen, this is true,
I am that Jesus whom they slew.'

And shadows dim, I dreamed, the dead apostles came,
And bent their heads for sorrow and for shame—
Sorrow for their great loss, and shame
For what they did in that vain name.

And in long ranges far behind there seemed
Pale vapoury angel forms; or was it cloud? that kept
Strange watch; the women also stood beside and wept.
   And Peter spoke the word: 20
'O my own Lord,
What is it we must do?
Is it then all untrue?
Did we not see, and hear, and handle Thee,

31

Yea, for whole hours
Upon the Mount in Galilee,
On the lake shore, and here at Bethany,
When Thou ascendedst to Thy God and ours?'

And paler still became the distant cloud,
And at the word the women wept aloud.   30

And the Shade answered, 'What ye say I know not;
        But it is true
        I am that Jesus whom they slew,
Whom ye have preached, but in what way I know not.'

        *   *   *   *   *

And the great World, it chanced, came by that way,
And stopped, and looked, and spoke to the police,
And said the thing, for order's sake and peace,
Most certainly must be suppressed, the nuisance cease.
His wife and daughter must have where to pray,
And whom to pray to, at the least one day   40
In seven, and something sensible to say.

Whether the fact so many years ago
Had, or not, happened, how was he to know?
Yet he had always heard that it was so.
As for himself, perhaps it was all one;
And yet he found it not unpleasant, too,
On Sunday morning in the roomy pew,
To see the thing with such decorum done.
As for himself, perhaps it was all one;
Yet on one's death-bed all men always said   50
It was a comfortable thing to think upon
The atonement and the resurrection of the dead.
So the great World as having said his say,

Unto his country-house pursued his way.
And on the grave the Shadow sat all day.

* * * * *

And the poor Pope was sure it must be so,
Else wherefore did the people kiss his toe?
The subtle Jesuit cardinal shook his head,
And mildly looked and said,
It mattered not a jot   60
Whether the thing, indeed, were so or not;
Religion must be kept up, and the Church preserved,
And for the people this best served,
And then he turned, and added most demurely,
'Whatever may befal,
We Catholics need no evidence at all,
The holy father is infallible, surely!'

And English canons heard,
And quietly demurred.
Religion rests on evidence, of course,   70
And on inquiry we must put no force.
Difficulties still, upon whatever ground,
Are likely, almost certain, to be found.
The Theist scheme, the Pantheist, one and all,
Must with, or e'en before, the Christian fall.
And till the thing were plainer to our eyes,
To disturb faith was surely most unwise.
As for the Shade, who trusted such narration?
Except, of course, in ancient revelation.

And dignitaries of the Church came by.   80
It had been worth to some of them, they said,
Some hundred thousand pounds a year a head.
If it fetched so much in the market, truly,
'Twas not a thing to be given up unduly.

33

It had been proved by Butler in one way,
By Paley better in a later day;
It had been proved in twenty ways at once,
By many a doctor plain to many a dunce;
There was no question but it must be so.
    And the Shade answered, that He did not know;   90
He had no reading, and might be deceived,
But still He was the Christ, as He believed.

And women, mild and pure,
Forth from still homes and village schools did pass,
And asked, if this indeed were thus, alas,
What should they teach their children and the poor?
    The Shade replied, He could not know,
But it was truth, the fact was so.

★　　★　　★　　★
★　　★　　★　　★

Who had kept all commandments from his youth
Yet still found one thing lacking—even Truth: 100
And the Shade only answered, 'Go, make haste,
Enjoy thy great possessions as thou may'st.'

The Latest Decalogue

Thou shalt have one God only; who
Would be at the expense of two?
No graven images may be
Worshipped, except the currency:
Swear not at all; for, for thy curse
Thine enemy is none the worse:
At church on Sunday to attend
Will serve to keep the world thy friend:

Honour thy parents; that is, all
From whom advancement may befall;   10
Thou shalt not kill; but need'st not strive
Officiously to keep alive:
Do not adultery commit;
Advantage rarely comes of it:
Thou shalt not steal; an empty feat,
When it's so lucrative to cheat:
Bear not false witness; let the lie
Have time on its own wings to fly:
Thou shalt not covet, but tradition
Approves all forms of competition.   20

From

The Bothie of Tober-na-Vuolich

Elspie's Answer to Philip

                              Well,—she answered,
And she was silent some time, and blushed all over,
    and answered
Quietly, after her fashion, still knitting, Maybe, I think of it,
Though I don't know that I did: and she paused again; but
    it may be,
Yes,—I don't know, Mr Philip,—but only it feels to me strangely,
Like to the high new bridge, they used to build at, below there
Over the burn and glen on the road. You won't understand me.
But I keep saying in my mind—this long time slowly with trouble
I have been building myself, up, up, and toilfully raising,
Just like as if the bridge were to do it itself without masons,   10
Painfully getting myself upraised one stone on another,

35

All one side I mean; and now I see on the other
Just such another fabric uprising, better and stronger,
Close to me, coming to join me: and then I sometimes fancy,—
Sometimes I find myself dreaming at nights about arches and
    bridges,—
Sometimes I dream of a great invisible hand coming down, and
Dropping the great key-stone in the middle: there in my dreaming,
There I felt the great key-stone coming in, and through it
Feel the other part—all the other stones of the archway,
Joined into mine with a strange happy sense of completeness.
    But, dear me,   20
This is confusion and nonsense. I mix all the things I can think of.
And you won't understand, Mr Philip.

From

Amours de Voyage

CLAUDE TO EUSTACE

I

DEAR EUSTATIO, I write that you may write me an answer,
Or at the least to put us again *en rapport* with each other.
Rome disappoints me much,—St Peter's, perhaps, in especial;
Only the Arch of Titus and view from the Lateran please me:
This, however, perhaps is the weather, which truly is horrid.
Greece must be better, surely; and yet I am feeling so spiteful,
That I could travel to Athens, to Delphi, and Troy, and
    Mount Sinai,
Though but to see with my eyes that these are vanity also.
    Rome disappoints me much; I hardly as yet understand, but
Rubbishy seems the word that most exactly would suit it.   10
All the foolish destructions, and all the sillier savings,

36

All the incongruous things of past incompatible ages,
Seem to be treasured up here to make fools of present and future.
Would to Heaven the old Goths had made a cleaner sweep of it!
Would to Heaven some new ones would come and destroy
        these churches!
However, one can live in Rome as also in London.
It is a blessing, no doubt, to be rid, at least for a time, of
All one's friends and relations,—yourself (forgive me!)
        included,—
All the *assujettissement* of having been what one has been,
What one thinks one is, or thinks that others suppose one;   20
Yet, in despite of all, we turn like fools to the English.
Vernon has been my fate; who is here the same that you
        knew him,—
Making the tour, it seems, with friends of the name of Trevellyn.

II

ROME disappoints me still; but I shrink and adapt myself to it.
Somehow a tyrannous sense of a superincumbent oppression
Still, wherever I go, accompanies ever, and makes me
Feel like a tree (shall I say?) buried under a ruin of brickwork.
Rome, believe me, my friend, is like its own Monte Testaceo,
Merely a marvellous mass of broken and castaway wine-pots.
Ye gods! what do I want with this rubbish of ages departed,   30
Things that Nature abhors, the experiments that she has failed in?
What do I find in the Forum? An archway and two or three
        pillars.
Well, but St Peter's? Alas, Bernini has filled it with sculpture!
No one can cavil, I grant, at the size of the great Coliseum.
Doubtless the notion of grand and capacious and massive
        amusement,
This the old Romans had; but tell me, is this an idea?
Yet of solidity much, but of splendour little is extant:
'Brickwork I found thee, and marble I left thee!' their
        Emperor vaunted;

'Marble I thought thee, and brickwork I find thee!' the Tourist
    may answer.

III

Dulce it is, and *decorum,* no doubt, for the country to fall,—to   40
Offers one's blood an oblation to Freedom, and die for the
    Cause; yet
Still, individual culture is also something, and no man
Finds quite distinct the assurance that he of all others is called on,
Or would be justified even, in taking away from the world that
Precious creature, himself. Nature sent him here to abide here;
Else why send him at all? Nature wants him still, it is likely;
On the whole, we are meant to look after ourselves; it is certain
Each has to eat for himself, digest for himself, and in general
Care for his own dear life, and see to his own preservation;
Nature's intentions, in most things uncertain, in this are decisive; 50
Which, on the whole, I conjecture the Romans will follow, and
    I shall.

  So we cling to our rocks like limpets; Ocean may bluster,
Over and under and round us; we open our shells to imbibe our
Nourishment, close them again, and are safe, fulfilling the purpose
Nature intended,—a wise one, of course, and a noble, we doubt not.
Sweet it may be and decorous, perhaps, for the country to die; but,
On the whole, we conclude the Romans won't do it, and I sha'n't.

IV

Now supposing the French or the Neapolitan soldier
Should by some evil chance come exploring the Maison Serny
(Where the family English are all to assemble for safety),   60
Am I prepared to lay down my life for the British female?
Really, who knows? One has bowed and talked, till, little by little,
All the natural heat has escaped of the chivalrous spirit.
Oh, one conformed, of course; but one doesn't die for good
    manners,
Stab or shoot, or be shot, by way of graceful attention.
No, if it should be at all, it should be on the barricades there;

Should I incarnadine ever this inky pacifical finger,
Sooner far should it be for this vapour of Italy's freedom,
Sooner far by the side of the d——d and dirty plebeians.
Ah, for a child in the street I could strike; for the full-blown
    lady——   70
Somehow, Eustace, alas! I have not felt the vocation.
Yet these people of course will expect, as of course, my protection,
Vernon in radiant arms stand forth for the lovely Georgina,
And to appear, I suppose, were but common civility. Yes, and
Truly I do not desire they should either be killed or offended.
Oh, and of course, you will say, 'When the time comes, you
    will be ready'.
Ah, but before it comes, am I to presume it will be so?
What I cannot feel now, am I to suppose that I shall feel?
Am I not free to attend for the ripe and indubious instinct?
Am I forbidden to wait for the clear and lawful perception?   80
Is it the calling of man to surrender his knowledge and insight,
For the mere venture of what may, perhaps, be the virtuous action?
Must we, walking our earth, discern a little, and hoping
Some plain visible task shall yet for our hands be assigned us,—
Must we abandon the future for fear of omitting the present,
Quit our own fireside hopes at the alien call of a neighbour,
To the mere possible shadow of Deity offer the victim?
And is all this, my friend, but a weak and ignoble refining,
Wholly unworthy the head or the heart of Your Own
    Correspondent?

                                          V

THERE are two different kinds, I believe, of human attraction: 90
One which simply disturbs, unsettles, and makes you uneasy,
And another that poises, retains, and fixes and holds you.
I have no doubt, for myself, in giving my voice for the latter.
I do not wish to be moved, but growing where I was growing,
There more truly to grow, to live where as yet I had languished.
I do not like being moved: for the will is excited; and action

                                          39

Is a most dangerous thing; I tremble for something factitious,
Some malpractice of heart and illegitimate process;
We are so prone to these things, with our terrible notions of duty.

There is no God

'There is no God,' the wicked saith,
  'And truly it's a blessing,
For what He might have done with us
  It's better only guessing.'

'There is no God', a youngster thinks,
  'Or really, if there may be,
He surely didn't mean a man
  Always to be a baby.'

'There is no God, or if there is,'
  The tradesman thinks, ' 'twere funny   10
If He should take it ill in me
  To make a little money.'

'Whether there be,' the rich man says,
  'It matters very little,
For I and mine, thank somebody,
  Are not in want of victual.'

Some others, also, to themselves,
  Who scarce so much as doubt it,
Think there is none, when they are well,
  And do not think about it.   20

But country folks who live beneath
  The shadow of the steeple;
The parson and the parson's wife,
  And mostly married people;

Youths green and happy in first love,
    So thankful for illusion;
And men caught out in what the world
    Calls guilt, in first confusion;

And almost every one when age,
    Disease, or sorrows strike him,   30
Inclines to think there is a God,
    Or something very like Him.

Spectator ab Extra

I

As I sat in the Café I said to myself,
They may talk as they please about what they call pelf,
They may sneer as they like about eating and drinking,
But help it I cannot, I cannot help thinking
    How pleasant it is to have money, heigh-ho!
    How pleasant it is to have money.

I sit at my table *en grand seigneur*,
And when I have done, throw a crust to the poor;
Not only the pleasure itself of good living,
But also the pleasure of now and then giving: 10
    So pleasant it is to have money, heigh-ho!
    So pleasant it is to have money.

They may talk as they please about what they call pelf,
And how one ought never to think of one's self,
How pleasures of thought surpass eating and drinking,—
My pleasure of thought is the pleasure of thinking
    How pleasant it is to have money, heigh-ho!
    How pleasant it is to have money.

Le Diner

Come along, 'tis the time, ten or more minutes past,
And he who came first had to wait for the last;   20
The oysters ere this had been in and been out;
Whilst I have been sitting and thinking about
    How pleasant it is to have money, heigh-ho!
    How pleasant it is to have money.

A clear soup with eggs; *voilà tout*; of the fish
The *filets de sole* are a moderate dish
À la Orly, but you're for red mullet, you say:
By the gods of good fare, who can question today
    How pleasant it is to have money, heigh-ho!
    How pleasant it is to have money.   30

After oysters, sauterne; then sherry; champagne,
Ere one bottle goes, comes another again;
Fly up, thou bold cork, to the ceiling above,
And tell to our ears in the sound that they love
    How pleasant it is to have money, heigh-ho!
    How pleasant it is to have money.

I've the simplest of palates; absurd it may be,
But I almost could dine on a *poulet-au-riz*,
Fish and soup and omelette and that—but the deuce—
There were to be woodcocks, and not *Charlotte Russe*!   40
    So pleasant it is to have money, heigh-ho!
    So pleasant it is to have money.

Your chablis is acid, away with the hock,
Give me the pure juice of the purple médoc:
St Péray is exquisite; but, if you please,
Some burgundy just before tasting the cheese.

So pleasant it is to have money, heigh-ho!
So pleasant it is to have money.

As for that, pass the bottle, and d——n the expense,
I've seen it observed by a writer of sense,   50
That the labouring classes could scarce live a day,
If people like us didn't eat, drink, and pay.
    So useful it is to have money, heigh-ho!
    So useful it is to have money.

One ought to be grateful, I quite apprehend,
Having dinner and supper and plenty to spend,
And so suppose now, while the things go away,
By way of a grace we stand up and say
    How pleasant it is to have money, heigh-ho!
    How pleasant it is to have money.   60

III

Parvenant

I cannot but ask, in the park and the streets
When I look at the number of persons one meets,
What e'er in the world the poor devils can do
Whose fathers and mothers can't give them a *sous*.
    So needful it is to have money, heigh-ho!
    So needful it is to have money.

I ride, and I drive, and I care not a d——n,
The people look up and they ask who I am;
And if I should chance to run over a cad,
I can pay for the damage, if ever so bad.   70
    So useful it is to have money, heigh-ho!
    So useful it is to have money.

It was but this winter I came up to town,
And already I'm gaining a sort of renown;

43

Find my way to good houses without much ado,
Am beginning to see the nobility too.
　　So useful it is to have money, heigh-ho!
　　So useful it is to have money.

O dear what a pity they ever should lose it,
Since they are the people that know how to use it;　　80
So easy, so stately, such manners, such dinners,
And yet, after all, it is we are the winners.
　　So needful it is to have money, heigh-ho!
　　So needful it is to have money.

It's all very well to be handsome and tall,
Which certainly makes you look well at a ball;
It's all very well to be clever and witty,
But if you are poor, why it's only a pity.
　　So needful it is to have money, heigh-ho!
　　So needful it is to have money.　　90

There's something undoubtedly in a fine air,
To know how to smile and be able to stare,
High breeding is something, but well-bred or not
In the end the one question is, what have you got.
　　So needful it is to have money, heigh-ho!
　　So needful it is to have money.

And the angels in pink and the angels in blue,
In muslins and moirés so lovely and new,
What is it they want, and so wish you to guess,
But if you have money, the answer is Yes.　　100
　　So needful, they tell you, is money, heigh-ho!
　　So needful it is to have money.

MATTHEW ARNOLD

From

The Strayed Reveller

The Gods are happy
They turn on all sides
Their shining eyes:
And see, below them,
The Earth, and men.

They see Tiresias
Sitting, staff in hand,
On the warm, grassy
Asopus bank:
His robe drawn over   10
His old, sightless head,
Revolving inly
The doom of Thebes.

They see the Centaurs
In the upper glens
Of Pelion, in the streams,
Where red-berried ashes fringe
The clear-brown shallow pools,
With streaming flanks, and heads
Rear'd proudly, snuffing   20
The mountain wind.
They see the Indian

Drifting, knife in hand,
His frail boat moor'd to
A floating isle thick-matted
With large leaved, low-creeping melon-plants,
And the dark cucumber.
He reaps, and stows them,
Drifting—drifting;—round him,
Round his green harvest-plot,   30
Flow the cool lake-waves,
The mountains ring them.

They see the Scythian
On the wide stepp, unharnessing
His wheel'd house at noon.
He tethers his beast down, and makes his meal—
Mare's milk, and bread
Baked on the embers:—all round
The boundless, waving grass-plains stretch, thick-starr'd
With saffron and the yellow hollyhock   40
And flag-leaved iris-flowers.
Sitting in his cart
He makes his meal; before him, for long miles,
Alive with bright green lizards,
And the springing bustard fowl,
The track, a straight black line,
Furrows the rich soil; here and there
Clusters of lonely mounds
Topp'd with rough-hewn,
Grey, rain-blear'd statues, overpeer   50
The sunny waste.
They see the ferry
On the broad, clay-laden
Lone Chorasmian stream:—thereon,
With snort and strain,
Two horses, strongly swimming, tow

The ferry boat, with woven ropes
To either bow
Firm-harness'd by the mane; a chief,
With shout and shaken spear   60
Stands at the prow, and guides them: but astern,
The cowering merchants, in long robes,
Sit pale beside their wealth
Of silk-bales and of balsam-drops,
Of gold and ivory,
Of turquoise-earth and amethyst,
Jasper and chalcedony,
And milk-barr'd onyx stones.
The loaded boat swings groaning
In the yellow eddies;   70
The Gods behold them.

They see the Heroes
Sitting in the dark ship
On the foamless, long-heaving,
Violent sea:
At sunset nearing
The Happy Islands.

These things, Ulysses,
The wise bards also
Behold and sing.   80
But oh, what labour!
O prince, what pain!

They too can see
Tiresias:—but the Gods,
Who give them vision,
Added this law:
That they should bear too
His groping blindness,

His dark foreboding,
His scorn'd white hairs;
Bear Hera's anger
Through a life lengthen'd
To seven ages.

They see the Centaurs
On Pelion;—then they feel,
They too, the maddening wine
Swell their large veins to bursting; in wild pain
They feel the biting spears
Of the grim Lapithæ, and Theseus, drive,
Drive crashing through their bones: they feel 100
High on a jutting rock in the red stream
Alcmena's dreadful son
Ply his bow;—such a price
The Gods exact for song:
To become what we sing.

They see the Indian
On his mountain lake; but squalls
Make their skiff reel, and worms
In the unkind spring have gnaw'd
Their melon-harvest to the heart.—They see
The Scythian; but long frosts
Parch them in winter-time on the bare Stepp,
Till they too fade like grass; they crawl
Like shadows forth in spring.

They see the Merchants
On the Oxus stream;—but care
Must visit first them too, and make them pale.
Whether, through whirling sand,
A cloud of desert robber-horse have burst
Upon their caravan; or greedy kings, 120

In the wall'd cities the way passes through,
Crush'd them with tolls; or fever-airs,
On some great river's marge,
Mown them down, far from home.

They see the Heroes
Near harbour;—but they share
Their lives, and former violent toil in Thebes,
Seven-gated Thebes, or Troy:
Or where the echoing oars
Of Argo first   130
Startled the unknown sea.

The old Silenus
Came, lolling in the sunshine,
From the dewy forest-coverts,
This way, at noon.
Sitting by me, while his Fauns
Down at the water side
Sprinkled and smoothed
His drooping garland,
He told me these things.   140

But I, Ulysses,
Sitting on the warm steps,
Looking over the valley,
All day long, have seen,
Without pain, without labour,
Sometimes a wild-hair'd Mænad—
Sometimes a Faun with torches—
And sometimes, for a moment,
Passing through the dark stems
Flowing-robed,—the beloved,
The desired, the divine,
Beloved Iacchus.

Human Life

What mortal, when he saw,
Life's voyage done, his heavenly friend,
Could ever yet dare tell him fearlessly:
'I have kept uninfringed my nature's law.
The inly-written chart thou gavest me,
To guide me, I have steer'd by to the end'?

Ah! let us make no claim
On life's incognisable sea
To too exact a steering of our way;
Let us not fret and fear to miss our aim   10
If some fair coast has lured us to make stay,
Or some friend hail'd us to keep company.

Ay! we would each fain drive
At random, and not steer by rule.
Weakness! and worse, weakness bestow'd in vain!
Winds from our side the unsuiting consort rive:
We rush by coasts where he had lief remain;
Man cannot, though he would, live chance's fool.

No! as the foaming swath
Of torn-up water, on the main,   20
Falls heavily away with long-drawn roar
On either side the black deep-furrow'd path
Cut by an onward-labouring vessel's prore,
And never touches the ship-side again;

Even so we leave behind,
As, charter'd by some unknown Powers,

We stem across the sea of life by night,
The joys which were not for our use design'd;—
The friends to whom we had no natural right,
The homes that were not destined to be ours.   30

Isolation

Yes! in the sea of life enisled,
With echoing straits between us thrown,
Dotting the shoreless watery wild,
We mortal millions live *alone*.
The islands feel the enclasping flow,
And then their endless bounds they know.

But when the moon their hollows lights,
And they are swept by balms of spring,
And in their glens, on starry nights,
The nightingales divinely sing;   10
And lovely notes, from shore to shore,
Across the sounds and channels pour—

Oh! then a longing like despair
Is to their farthest caverns sent;
For surely once, they feel, we were
Parts of a single continent!
Now round us spreads the watery plain—
Oh might our marges meet again!

Who order'd, that their longing's fire
Should be, as soon as kindled, cool'd?   20
Who renders vain their deep desire?—
A God, a God their severance ruled!
And bade betwixt their shores to be
The unplumb'd, salt, estranging sea.

Dover Beach

The sea is calm tonight,
The tide is full, the moon lies fair
Upon the straits;—on the French coast the light
Gleams, and is gone; the cliffs of England stand,
Glimmering and vast, out in the tranquil bay.
Come to the window, sweet is the night-air!
Only, from the long line of spray
Where the sea meets the moon-blanch'd land,
Listen! you hear the grating roar
Of pebbles which the waves draw back, and fling,   10
At their return, up the high strand,
Begin, and cease, and then again begin,
With tremulous cadence slow, and bring
The eternal note of sadness in.

Sophocles long ago
Heard it on the Ægæan, and it brought
Into his mind the turbid ebb and flow
Of human misery; we
Find also in the sound a thought,
Hearing it by this distant northern sea.   20

The Sea of Faith
Was once, too, at the full, and round earth's shore
Lay like the folds of a bright girdle furl'd.
But now I only hear
Its melancholy, long, withdrawing roar,
Retreating, to the breath
Of the night-wind down the vast edges drear
And naked shingles of the world.

Ah, love, let us be true
To one another! for the world, which seems   30
To lie before us like a land of dreams,
So various, so beautiful, so new,
Hath really neither joy, nor love, nor light,
Nor certitude, nor peace, nor help for pain;
And we are here as on a darkling plain
Swept with confused alarms of struggle and flight,
Where ignorant armies clash by night.

From

Stanzas from the Grande Chartreuse

Those halls too, destined to contain
Each its own pilgrim-host of old,
From England, Germany, or Spain—
All are before me! I behold
The House, the Brotherhood austere!
—And what am I, that I am here?

For rigorous teachers seized my youth,
And purg'd its faith, and trimm'd its fire,
Show'd me the high, white star of Truth,
There bade me gaze, and there aspire.   10
Even now their whispers pierce the gloom:
What dost thou in this living tomb?

Forgive me, masters of the mind!
At whose behest I long ago
So much unlearnt, so much resign'd—
I come not here to be your foe!

I seek these anchorites, not in ruth,
To curse and to deny you truth;

Not as their friend, or child, I speak!
But as, on some far northern strand,   20
Thinking of his own Gods, a Greek
In pity and mournful awe might stand
Before some fallen Runic stone—
For both were faiths, and both are gone.

Wandering between two worlds, one dead,
The other powerless to be born,
With nowhere yet to rest my head,
Like these, on earth I wait forlorn.
Their faith, my tears, the world deride—
I come to shed them at their side.   30

Oh, hide me in your gloom profound,
Ye solemn seats of holy pain!
Take me, cowl'd forms, and fence me round
Till I possess my soul again;
Till free my thoughts before me roll,
Not chafed by hourly false control!

For the world cries your faith is now
But a dead time's exploded dream;
My melancholy, sciolists say,
Is a pass'd mode, an outworn theme—   40
As if the world had ever had
A faith, or sciolists been sad!

Ah, if it *be* pass'd, take away,
At least, the restlessness, the pain!
Be man henceforth no more a prey
To these out-dated stings again!

The nobleness of grief is gone—
Ah, leave us not the fret alone!

But—if you cannot give us ease—
Last of the race of them who grieve   50
Here leave us to die out with these
Last of the people who believe!
Silent, while years engrave the brow;
Silent—the best are silent now.

Achilles ponders in his tent,
The kings of modern thought are dumb;
Silent they are, though not content,
And wait to see the future come.
They have the grief men had of yore,
But they contend and cry no more.   60

Our fathers water'd with their tears
This sea of time whereon we sail,
Their voices were in all men's ears
Who pass'd within their puissant hail.
Still the same ocean round us raves,
But we stand mute, and watch the waves.

For what avail'd it, all the noise
And outcry of the former men?—
Say, have their sons achieved more joys?
Say, is life lighter now than then?   70
The sufferers died, they left their pain—
The pangs which tortured them remain.

What helps it now, that Byron bore,
With haughty scorn which mock'd the smart,
Through Europe to the Aetolian shore
The pageant of his bleeding heart?

That thousands counted every groan,
And Europe made his woe her own?

What boots it, Shelley! that the breeze
Carried thy lovely wail away,   80
Musical through Italian trees
Which fringe thy soft blue Spezzian bay?
Inheritors of thy distress
Have restless hearts one throb the less?

The Scholar-Gipsy

There was very lately a lad in the University of Oxford, who was by his
poverty forced to leave his studies there; and at last to join himself to a company of vagabond gipsies. Among these extravagant people, by the insinuat-
ing subtilty of his carriage, he quickly got so much of their love and esteem
as that they discovered to him their mystery. After he had been a pretty
while well exercised in the trade, there chanced to ride by a couple of scholars,
who had formerly been of his acquaintance. They quickly spied out their old
friend among the gipsies; and he gave them an account of the necessity which
drove him to that kind of life, and told them that the people he went with
were not such impostors as they were taken for, but that they had a traditional kind of learning among them, and could do wonders by the power of
imagination, their fancy binding that of others: that himself had learned much
of their art, and when he had compassed the whole secret, he intended, he
said, to leave their company, and give the world an account of what he had
learned.—GLANVIL's *Vanity of Dogmatizing*, 1661.

Go, for they call you, Shepherd, from the hill;
   Go, Shepherd, and untie the wattled cotes:
      No longer leave thy wistful flock unfed,
   Nor let thy bawling fellows rack their throats,
      Nor the cropp'd herbage shoot another head.
         But when the fields are still,

56

And the tired men and dogs all gone to rest,
  And only the white sheep are sometimes seen
  Cross and recross the strips of moon-blanch'd green,
    Come, Shepherd, and again renew the quest!   10

Here, where the reaper was at work of late—
  In this high field's dark corner, where he leaves
  His coat, his basket, and his earthen cruse,
  And in the sun all morning binds the sheaves,
    Then here, at noon, comes back his stores to use—
      Here will I sit and wait,
  While to my ear from uplands far away
  The bleating of the folded flocks is borne,
  With distant cries of reapers in the corn—
    All the live murmur of a summer's day.   20

Screen'd is this nook o'er the high, half-reap'd field,
  And here till sun-down, shepherd! will I be.
  Through the thick corn the scarlet poppies peep
  And round green roots and yellowing stalks I see
    Pale pink convolvulus in tendrils creep;
      And air-swept lindens yield
  Their scent, and rustle down their perfumed showers
  Of bloom on the bent grass where I am laid,
  And bower me from the August sun with shade;
    And the eye travels down to Oxford's towers.   30

And near me on the grass lies Glanvil's book—
  Come, let me read the oft-read tale again!
  The story of that Oxford scholar poor,
  Of pregnant parts and quick inventive brain,
    Who, tired of knocking at preferment's door,
      One summer-morn forsook
  His friends, and went to learn the gipsy-lore,
  And roam'd the world with that wild brotherhood,

S.V.P.—5   57

And came, as most men deem'd, to little good,
   But came to Oxford and his friends no more.   40

But once, years after, in the country lanes,
   Two scholars whom at college erst he knew
   Met him, and of his way of life enquired;
   Whereat he answer'd, that the gipsy-crew,
     His mates, had arts to rule as they desired
      The workings of men's brains,
And they can bind them to what thoughts they will.
   'And I,' he said, 'the secret of their art,
    When fully learn'd, will to the world impart:
     But it needs heaven-sent moments for this skill.'   50

This said, he left them, and return'd no more.—
   But rumours hung about the country-side,
   That the lost Scholar long was seen to stray,
   Seen by rare glimpses, pensive and tongue-tied,
     In hat of antique shape, and cloak of grey,
      The same the gipsies wore.
Shepherds had met him on the Hurst in spring;
   At some lone alehouse in the Berkshire moors,
   On the warm ingle bench, the smock-frock'd boors
    Had found him seated at their entering,   60

But, 'mid their drink and clatter, he would fly.
   And I myself seem half to know thy looks,
   And put the shepherds, wanderer! on thy trace;
   And boys who in lone wheatfields scare the rooks
     I ask if thou hast pass'd their quiet place;
      Or in my boat I lie
Moor'd to the cool bank in the summer heats,
   'Mid wide grass meadows which the sunshine fills,
   And watch the warm, green-muffled Cumner hills,
    And wonder if thou haunt'st their shy retreats.   70

For most, I know, thou lov'st retired ground!
  Thee, at the ferry, Oxford riders blithe,
    Returning home on summer nights, have met
  Crossing the stripling Thames at Bab-lock-hithe,
    Trailing in the cool stream thy fingers wet,
      As the punt's rope chops round:
  And leaning backwards in a pensive dream,
    And fostering in thy lap a heap of flowers
    Pluck'd in shy fields and distant Wychwood bowers,
      And thine eyes resting on the moonlit stream.   80

And then they land, and thou art seen no more!—
  Maidens, who from the distant hamlets come
    To dance around the Fyfield elm in May,
  Oft through the darkening fields have seen thee roam,
    Or cross a stile into the public way.
      Oft thou hast given them store
  Of flowers—the frail-leaf'd, white anemony—
    Dark bluebells drench'd with dews of summer eves,
    And purple orchises with spotted leaves—
      But none has words she can report of thee.   90

And, above Godstow Bridge, when hay-time's here
  In June, and many a scythe in sunshine flames,
    Men who through those wide fields of breezy grass
  Where black-wing'd swallows haunt the glittering Thames,
    To bathe in the abandon'd lasher pass,
      Have often pass'd thee near
  Sitting upon the river bank o'ergrown;
    Mark'd thine outlandish garb, thy figure spare,
    Thy dark vague eyes, and soft abstracted air;
      But, when they came from bathing, thou wast gone! 100

At some lone homestead in the Cumner hills,
  Where at her open door the housewife darns,

Thou hast been seen, or hanging on a gate
To watch the threshers in the mossy barns.
 Children, who early range these slopes and late
  For cresses from the rills,
Have known thee eying, all an April-day,
 The springing pastures and the feeding kine;
 And mark'd thee, when the stars come out and shine,
  Through the long dewy grass move slow away.   110

In autumn, on the skirts of Bagley Wood—
 Where most the gipsies by the turf-edged way
  Pitch their smoked tents, and every bush you see
With scarlet patches tagg'd and shreds of grey,
 Above the forest ground call'd Thessaly—
  The blackbird, picking food
Sees thee, nor stops his meal, nor fears at all;
 So often has he known thee past him stray
 Rapt, twirling in thy hand a wither'd spray,
  And waiting for the spark from heaven to fall.   120

And once, in winter, on the causeway chill
 Where home through flooded fields foot-travellers go,
  Have I not pass'd thee on the wooden bridge,
Wrapt in thy cloak and battling with the snow,
 Thy face tow'rd Hinksey and its wintry ridge?
  And thou hast climb'd the hill,
And gain'd the white brow of the Cumner range;
 Turn'd once to watch, while thick the snowflakes fall,
 The line of festal light in Christ-Church hall—
  Then sought thy straw in some sequester'd grange.   130

But what—I dream! Two hundred years are flown
 Since first thy story ran through Oxford halls,
  And the grave Glanvil did the tale inscribe
That thou wert wander'd from the studious walls

To learn strange arts, and join a gipsy-tribe:
        And thou from earth art gone
Long since, and in some quiet churchyard laid—
        Some country-nook, where o'er thy unknown grave
        Tall grasses and white flowering nettles wave—
                Under a dark, red-fruited yew-tree's shade.   140

—No, no, thou hast not felt the lapse of hours!
    For what wears out the life of mortal men?
        'Tis that from change to change their being rolls:
        'Tis that repeated shocks, again, again,
            Exhaust the energy of strongest souls
                And numb the elastic powers.
    Till having used our nerves with bliss and teen,
        And tired upon a thousand schemes our wit,
            To the just-pausing Genius we remit
                Our worn-out life, and are—what we have been.   150

Thou hast not lived, why should'st thou perish, so?
    Thou hadst *one* aim, *one* business, *one* desire:
        Else wert thou long since number'd with the dead—
        Else hadst thou spent, like other men, thy fire.
            The generations of thy peers are fled,
                And we ourselves shall go;
    But thou possessest an immortal lot,
        And we imagine thee exempt from age
        And living as thou liv'st on Glanvil's page,
                Because thou hadst—what we, alas! have not.   160

For early didst thou leave the world, with powers
    Fresh, undiverted to the world without,
        Firm to their mark, not spent on other things;
        Free from the sick fatigue, the languid doubt,
            Which much to have tried, in much been baffled, brings.
                O life unlike to ours!

Who fluctuate idly without term or scope,
   Of whom each strives, nor knows for what he strives,
     And each half lives a hundred different lives;
      Who wait like thee, but not, like thee, in hope.   170

Thou waitest for the spark from heaven! and we,
   Light half-believers of our casual creeds,
     Who never deeply felt, nor clearly will'd,
     Whose insight never has borne fruit in deeds,
      Whose vague resolves never have been fulfill'd;
       For whom each year we see
   Breeds new beginnings, disappointments new;
     Who hesitate and falter life away,
     And lose tomorrow the ground won today—
      Ah! do not we, wanderer! await it too?   180

Yes, we await it!—but it still delays,
   And then we suffer; and among us one,
     Who most has suffer'd, takes dejectedly
   His seat upon the intellectual throne;
     And all his store of sad experience he
      Lays bare of wretched days;
   Tells us his misery's birth and growth and signs,
     And how the dying spark of hope was fed,
     And how the breast was sooth'd, and how the head,
      And all his hourly varied anodynes.   190

This for our wisest! and we others pine,
   And wish the long unhappy dream would end,
     And waive all claim to bliss, and try to bear
   With close-lipp'd patience for our only friend,
     Sad patience, too near neighbour to despair—
      But none has hope like thine!
   Thou through the fields and through the woods dost stray,
     Roaming the country-side, a truant boy,

Nursing thy project in unclouded joy,
  And every doubt long blown by time away.   200

O born in days when wits were fresh and clear,
  And life ran gaily as the sparkling Thames;
    Before this strange disease of modern life,
  With its sick hurry, its divided aims,
    Its heads o'ertax'd, its palsied hearts, was rife—
      Fly hence, our contact fear!
  Still fly, plunge deeper in the bowering wood!
    Averse, as Dido did with gesture stern
    From her false friend's approach in Hades turn,
      Wave us away, and keep thy solitude!   210

Still nursing the unconquerable hope,
  Still clutching the inviolable shade,
    With a free, onward impulse brushing through,
  By night, the silver'd branches of the glade—
    Far on the forest-skirts, where none pursue,
      On some mild pastoral slope
  Emerge, and resting on the moonlit pales
    Freshen thy flowers as in former years
    With dew, or listen with enchanted ears,
      From the dark dingles, to the nightingales!   220

But fly our paths, our feverish contact fly!
  For strong the infection of our mental strife,
    Which, though it gives no bliss, yet spoils for rest;
  And we should win thee from thy own fair life,
    Like us distracted, and like us unblest.
      Soon, soon thy cheer would die,
  Thy hopes grow timorous, and unfix'd thy powers,
    And thy clear aims be cross and shifting made;
    And then thy glad perennial youth would fade,
      Fade, and grow old at last and die like ours.   230

63

Then fly our greetings, fly our speech and smiles!
  —As some grave Tyrian trader, from the sea,
    Descried at sunrise an emerging prow
  Lifting the cool-hair'd creepers stealthily,
    The fringes of a southward-facing brow
      Among the Ægæan isles;
  And saw the merry Grecian coaster come,
    Freighted with amber grapes, and Chian wine,
    Green, bursting figs, and tunnies steep'd in brine—
      And knew the intruders on his ancient home,   240

The young light-hearted masters of the waves—
  And snatch'd his rudder, and shook out more sail;
    And day and night held on indignantly
  O'er the blue Midland waters with the gale,
    Betwixt the Syrtes and soft Sicily,
      To where the Atlantic raves
  Outside the western straits; and unbent sails
    There, where down cloudy cliffs, through sheets of foam,
    Shy traffickers, the dark Iberians come;
      And on the beach undid his corded bales.   250

Thyrsis

A MONODY

To commemorate the Author's friend, ARTHUR HUGH CLOUGH,
who died at Florence, 1861

How changed is here each spot man makes or fills!
  In the two Hinkseys nothing keeps the same;
    The village-street its haunted mansion lacks,

And from the sign is gone Sibylla's name,
    And from the roofs the twisted chimney-stacks—
        Are ye too changed, ye hills?
See, 'tis no foot of unfamiliar men
    Tonight from Oxford up your pathway strays!
        Here came I often, often, in old days—
Thyrsis and I; we still had Thyrsis then.   10

Runs it not here, the track by Childsworth Farm,
    Past the high wood, to where the elm-tree crowns
        The hill behind whose ridge the sunset flames?
The signal-elm, that looks on Ilsley Downs,
    The Vale, the three long weirs, the youthful Thames?—
        This winter-eve is warm,
Humid the air! leafless, yet soft as spring,
    The tender purple spray on copse and briers!
    And that sweet city with her dreaming spires,
She needs not June for beauty's heightening,   20

Lovely all times she lies, lovely tonight!—
    Only, methinks, some loss of habit's power
        Befalls me wandering through this upland dim.
Once pass'd I blindfold here, at any hour;
    Now seldom come I, since I came with him.
        That single elm-tree bright
Against the west—I miss it! is it gone?
    We prized it dearly; while it stood, we said,
    Our friend, the Gipsy-scholar, was not dead;
While the tree lived, he in these fields lived on.   30

Too rare, too rare, grow now my visits here,
    But once I knew each field, each flower, each stick;
        And with the country-folk acquaintance made
    By barn in threshing-time, by new-built rick.
        Here, too, our shepherd-pipes we first assay'd.

Ah me! this many a year
My pipe is lost, my shepherd's-holiday!
    Needs must I lose them, needs with heavy heart
    Into the world and wave of men depart;
But Thrysis of his own will went away.   40

It irk'd him to be here, he could not rest.
    He loved each simple joy the country yields,
        He loved his mates; but yet he could not keep,
    For that a shadow lour'd on the fields,
        Here with the shepherds and the silly sheep.
            Some life of men unblest
    He knew, which made him droop, and fill'd his head.
        He went; his piping took a troubled sound
        Of storms that rage outside our happy ground;
    He could not wait their passing, he is dead.   50

So, some tempestuous morn in early June,
    When the year's primal burst of bloom is o'er,
        Before the roses and the longest day—
    When garden-walks, and all the grassy floor
        With blossoms red and white of fallen May
            And chestnut-flowers are strewn—
    So have I heard the cuckoo's parting cry,
        From the wet field, through the vext garden-trees,
        Come with the volleying rain and tossing breeze:
    The bloom is gone, and with the bloom go I!   60

Too quick despairer, wherefore wilt thou go?
    Soon will the high Midsummer pomps come on,
        Soon will the musk carnations break and swell,
    Soon shall we have gold-dusted snapdragon,
        Sweet-William with his homely cottage-smell,
            And stocks in fragrant blow;
    Roses that down the alleys shine afar,

And open, jasmine-muffled lattices,
    And groups under the dreaming garden-trees,
And the full moon, and the white evening-star.   70

He hearkens not! light comer, he is flown!
    What matters it? next year he will return,
        And we shall have him in the sweet spring-days,
    With whitening hedges, and uncrumpling fern,
        And blue-bells trembling by the forest-ways,
            And scent of hay new-mown.
But Thrysis never more we swains shall see;
    See him come back, and cut a smoother reed,
    And blow a strain the world at last shall heed—
For Time, not Corydon, hath conquer'd thee.   80

Alack, for Corydon no rival now!—
    But when Sicilian shepherds lost a mate,
        Some good survivor with his flute would go,
    Piping a ditty sad for Bion's fate,
        And cross the unpermitted ferry's flow,
            And unbend Pluto's brow,
And make leap up with joy the beauteous head
    Of Proserpine, among whose crowned hair
    Are flowers first open'd on Sicilian air;
And flute his friend, like Orpheus, from the dead.   90

O easy access to the hearer's grace
    When Dorian shepherds sang to Proserpine!
        For she herself had trod Sicilian fields,
    She knew the Dorian water's gush divine,
        She knew each lily white which Enna yields,
            Each rose with blushing face;
She loved the Dorian pipe, the Dorian strain.
    But ah, of our poor Thames she never heard!

67

Her foot the Cumner cowslips never stirr'd;
And we should tease her with our plaint in vain!   100

Well! wind-dispersed and vain the words will be,
    Yet, Thrysis, let me give my grief its hour
        In the old haunt, and find our tree-topp'd hill!
    Who, if not I, for questing here hath power?
        I know the wood which hides the daffodil,
            I know the Fyfield tree,
    I know what white, what purple fritillaries
        The grassy harvest of the river-fields,
        Above by Ensham, down by Sandford, yields,
    And what sedged brooks are Thames's tributaries;   110

I know these slopes; who knows them if not I?—
    But many a dingle on the loved hill-side,
        With thorns once studded, old, white-blossom'd trees,
    Where thick the cowslips grew, and far descried
        High tower'd the spikes of purple orchises,
            Hath since our day put by
    The coronals of that forgotten time;
        Down each green bank hath gone the ploughboy's team,
        And only in the hidden brookside gleam
    Primroses, orphans of the flowery prime.   120

Where is the girl, who by the boatman's door,
    Above the locks, above the boating throng,
        Unmoor'd our skiff when through the Wytham flats,
    Red loosestrife and blond meadow-sweet among
        And darting swallows and light water-gnats,
            We track'd the shy Thames shore?
    Where are the mowers, who, as the tiny swell
        Of our boat passing heaved the river-grass,
        Stood with suspended scythe to see us pass?
    They all are gone, and thou art gone as well.   130

Yes, thou art gone! and round me too the night
  In ever-nearing circle weaves her shade.
    I see her veil draw soft across the day,
  I feel her slowly chilling breath invade
    The cheek grown thin, the brown hair sprent with grey;
      I feel her finger light
Laid pausefully upon life's headlong train;—
    The foot less prompt to meet the morning dew,
    The heart less bounding at emotion new,
And hope, once crush'd, less quick to spring again.   140

And long the way appears, which seem'd so short
  To the unpractised eye of sanguine youth;
    And high the mountain-tops, in cloudy air,
The mountain-tops where is the throne of Truth,
    Tops in life's morning-sun so bright and bare.
      Unbreachable the fort
Of the long-batter'd world uplifts its wall;
    And strange and vain the earthly turmoil grows,
    And near and real the charm of thy repose,
And night as welcome as a friend would fall.   150

But hush! the upland hath a sudden loss
  Of quiet!—Look, adown the dusk hillside,
    A troop of Oxford hunters going home,
As in old days, jovial and talking, ride!
    From hunting with the Berkshire hounds they come.
      Quick! let me fly, and cross
Into yon further field!—'Tis done; and see,
    Back'd by the sunset, which doth glorify
    The orange and pale violet evening-sky,
Bare on its lonely ridge, the Tree! the Tree!   160

I take the omen! Eve lets down her veil,
  The white fog creeps from bush to bush about,
69

The west unflushes, the high stars grow bright,
And in the scatter'd farms the lights come out.
  I cannot reach the signal-tree tonight,
      Yet, happy omen, hail!
  Hear it from thy broad lucent Arno-vale
    (For there thine earth-forgetting eyelids keep
    The morningless and unawakening sleep
  Under the flowery oleanders pale),   170

Hear it, O Thyrsis, still our tree is there!—
  Ah, vain! These English fields, this upland dim,
    These brambles pale with mist engarlanded,
  That lone, sky-pointing tree, are not for him.
      To a boon southern country he is fled,
        And now in happier air,
  Wandering with the great Mother's train divine
    (And purer or more subtle soul than thee,
    I trow, the mighty Mother doth not see)
  Within a folding of the Apennine,   180

Thou hearest the immortal strains of old!—
  Putting his sickle to the perilous grain
    In the hot cornfield of the Phrygian king,
  For thee the Lityerses-song again
      Young Daphnis with his silver voice doth sing;
        Sings his Sicilian fold,
  His sheep, his hapless love, his blinded eyes—
    And how a call celestial round him rang,
    And heavenward from the fountain-brink he sprang,
  And all the marvel of the golden skies.   190

There thou art gone, and me thou leavest here
  Sole in these fields! yet will I not despair.
    Despair I will not, while I yet descry
  Neath the mild canopy of English air

That lonely tree against the western sky.
  Still, still these slopes, 'tis clear,
Our Gipsy-Scholar haunts, outliving thee!
  Fields where soft sheep from cages pull the hay,
  Woods with anemonies in flower till May,
Know him a wanderer still; then why not me?   200

A fugitive and gracious light he seeks,
  Shy to illumine; and I seek it too.
    This does not come with houses or with gold,
  With place, with honour, and a flattering crew;
    'Tis not in the world's market bought and sold—
      But the smooth-slipping weeks
  Drop by, and leave its seeker still untired;
    Out of the heed of mortals he is gone,
    He wends unfollow'd, he must house alone;
  Yet on he fares, by his own heart inspired.   210

Thou too, O Thyrsis, on like quest wert bound;
  Thou wanderedst with me for a little hour!
    Men gave thee nothing; but this happy quest,
  If men esteem'd thee feeble, gave thee power,
    If men procured thee trouble, gave thee rest.
      And this rude Cumner ground,
  Its fir-topped Hurst, its farms, its quiet fields,
    Here cam'st thou in thy jocund youthful time,
    Here was thine height of strength, thy golden prime!
  And still the haunt beloved a virtue yields.   220

What though the music of thy rustic flute
  Kept not for long its happy, country tone;
    Lost it too soon, and learnt a stormy note
  Of men contention-tost, of men who groan,
    Which task'd thy pipe too sore, and tired thy throat—
      It fail'd, and thou wert mute.

Yet hadst thou always visions of our light,
   And long with men of care thou couldst not stay,
   And soon thy foot resumed its wandering way,
Left human haunt, and on alone till night.   230

Too rare, too rare, grow now my visits here!
   'Mid city-noise, not, as with thee of yore,
    Thyrsis! in reach of sheep-bells is my home.
   —Then through the great town's harsh, heart-wearying roar,
   Let in thy voice a whisper often come,
      To chase fatigue and fear:
Why faintest thou? I wander'd till I died.
   Roam on! The light we sought is shining still.
   Dost thou ask proof? Our tree yet crowns the hill,
Our Scholar travels yet the loved hill-side.   240

COVENTRY PATMORE

From

The Angel in the House

The Cathedral Close

Once more I came to Sarum Close,
    With joy half memory, half desire,
And breathed the sunny wind that rose
    And blew the shadows o'er the Spire,
And toss'd the lilac's scented plumes,
    And sway'd the chestnut's thousand cones,
And filled my nostrils with perfumes,
    And shaped the clouds in waifs and zones,
And wafted down the serious strain
    Of Sarum bells, when, true to time,   10
I reach'd the Dean's, with heart and brain
    That trembled to the trembling chime.

'Twas half my home, six years ago.
    The six years had not alter'd it:
Red-brick and ashlar, long and low,
    With dormers and with oriels lit.
Geranium, lychnis, rose array'd
    The windows, all wide open thrown;

And some one in the Study play'd
    The Wedding-March of Mendelssohn.   20
And there it was I last took leave:
    'Twas Christmas: I remember'd now
The cruel girls, who feign'd to grieve,
    Took down the evergreens; and how
The holly into blazes woke
    The fire, lighting the large, low room,
A dim, rich lustre of old oak
    And crimson velvet's glowing gloom.

No change had touch'd Dean Churchill: kind,
    By widowhood more than winters bent,   30
And settled in a cheerful mind,
    As still forecasting heaven's content.
Well might his thoughts be fix'd on high,
    Now she was there! Within her face
Humility and dignity
    Were met in a most sweet embrace.
She seem'd expressly sent below
    To teach our erring minds to see
The rhythmic change of time's swift flow
    As part of still eternity.   40
Her life, all honour, observed, with awe
    Which cross experience could not mar,
The fiction of the Christian law
    That all men honourable are;
And so her smile at once conferr'd
    High flattery and benign reproof;
And I, a rude boy, strangely stirr'd,
    Grew courtly in my own behoof.
The years, so far from doing her wrong,
    Anointed her with gracious balm,   50

And made her brows more and more young
  With wreaths of amaranth and palm.

Was this her eldest, Honor; prude,
  Who would not let me pull the swing;
Who, kiss'd at Christmas, call'd me rude,
  And, sobbing low, refused to sing?
How changed! In shape no slender Grace,
  But Venus; milder than the dove;
Her mother's air; her Norman face;
  Her large sweet eyes, clear lakes of love.   60
Mary I knew. In former time
  Ailing and pale, she thought that bliss
Was only for a better clime,
  And, heavenly overmuch, scorn'd this.
I, rash with theories of the right,
  Which stretch'd the tether of my Creed,
But did not break it, held delight
  Half discipline. We disagreed.
She told the Dean I wanted grace.
  Now she was kindest of the three,   70
And soft wild roses deck'd her face.
  And, what, was this my Mildred, she
To herself and all a sweet surprise?
  My Pet, who romp'd and roll'd a hoop?
I wonder'd where those daisy eyes
  Had found their touching curve and droop.

Unmannerly times! But now we sat
  Stranger than strangers; till I caught
And answer'd Mildred's smile; and that
  Spread to the rest, and freedom brought.   80

75

The Dean talk'd little, looking on,
    Of three such daughters justly vain.
What letters they had had from Bonn,
    Said Mildred, and what plums from Spain!
By Honor I was kindly task'd
    To excuse my never coming down
From Cambridge; Mary smiled and ask'd
    Were Kant and Goethe yet outgrown?
And, pleased, we talk'd the old days o'er;
    And, parting, I for pleasure sigh'd.   90
To be there as a friend, (since more),
    Seem'd then, seems still, excuse for pride;
For something that abode endued
    With temple-like repose, an air
Of life's kind purposes pursued
    With order'd freedom sweet and fair.
A tent pitch'd in a world not right
    It seem'd, whose inmates, every one,
On tranquil faces bore the light
    Of duties beautifully done,   100
And humbly, though they had few peers,
    Kept their own laws, which seem'd to be
The fair sum of six thousand years'
    Traditions of civility.

Honoria

Grown weary with a week's exile
    From those fair friends, I rode to see
The church-restorings; lounged awhile,
    And met the Dean; was ask'd to tea,

And found their cousin, Frederick Graham,
　　At Honor's side. Was I concern'd,
If, when she sang, his colour came,
　　That mine, as with a buffet, burn'd?
A man to please a girl! thought I,
　　Retorting his forced smiles, the shrouds　　　　　10
Of wrath, so hid as she was by,
　　Sweet moon between her lighted clouds!

Whether this Cousin was the cause
　　I know not, but I seem'd to see,
The first time then, how fair she was,
　　How much the fairest of the three.
Each stopp'd to let the other go;
　　But, time-bound, he arose the first.
Stay'd he in Sarum long? If so
　　I hoped to see him at the Hurst.　　　　　20
No: he had call'd here, on his way
　　To Portsmouth, where the Arrogant,
His ship, was; he should leave next day,
　　For two years' cruise in the Levant.

Had love in her yet struck its germs?
　　I watch'd. Her farewell show'd me plain
She loved, on the majestic terms
　　That she should not be loved again.
And so her cousin, parting, felt.
　　Hope in his voice and eye was dead.　　　　　30
Compassion did my malice melt;
　　Then went I home to a restless bed.
I, who admired her too, could see
　　His infinite remorse at this

77

Great mystery, that she should be
  So beautiful, yet not be his,
And, pitying, long'd to plead his part;
  But scarce could tell, so strange my whim,
Whether the weight upon my heart
  Was sorrow for myself or him.   40

She was all mildness; yet 'twas writ
  In all her grace, most legibly,
'He that's for heaven itself unfit,
  'Let him not hope to merit me.'
And such a challenge, quite apart
  From thoughts of love, humbled, and thus
To sweet repentance moved my heart,
  And made me more magnanimous,
And led me to review my life,
  Enquiring where in aught the least,   50
If question were of her for wife,
  Ill might be mended, hope increas'd.
Not that I soar'd so far above
  Myself, as this great hope to dare;
And yet I well foresaw that love
  Might hope where reason must despair;
And, half-resenting the sweet pride
  Which would not ask me to admire,
'Oh,' to my secret heart I sigh'd,
  'That I were worthy to desire!'   60

As drowsiness my brain reliev'd,
  A shrill defiance of all to arms,
Shriek'd by the stable-cock, receiv'd
  An angry answer from three farms.
And, then, I dream'd that I, her knight,

A clarion's haughty pathos heard,
And rode securely to the fight,
  Cased in the scarf she had conferr'd;
And there, the bristling lists behind,
  Saw many, and vanquish'd all I saw   70
Of her unnumber'd cousin-kind,
  In Navy, Army, Church, and Law;
Smitten, the warriors somehow turn'd
  To Sarum choristers, whose song,
Mix'd with celestial sorrow, yearn'd
  With joy no memory can prolong;
And phantasms as absurd and sweet
  Merged each in each in endless chace,
And everywhere I seem'd to meet
  The haunting fairness of her face.   80

Sahara

I stood by Honor and the Dean,
  They seated in the London train.
A month from her! yet this had been,
  Ere now, without such bitter pain.
But neighbourhood makes parting light,
  And distance remedy has none;
Alone, she near, I felt as might
  A blind man sitting in the sun;
She near, all for the time was well;
  Hope's self, when we were far apart,   10
With lonely feeling, like the smell
  Of heath on mountains, fill'd my heart.
To see her seem'd delight's full scope,
  And her kind smile, so clear of care,

Ev'n then, though darkening all my hope,
    Gilded the cloud of my despair.

She had forgot to bring a book.
    I lent one; blamed the print for old;
And did not tell her that she took
    A Petrarch worth its weight in gold.   20
I hoped she'd lose it; for my love
    Was grown so dainty, high, and nice,
It prized no luxury above
    The sense of fruitless sacrifice.

The bell rang, and, with shrieks like death,
    Link catching link, the long array,
With ponderous pulse and fiery breath,
    Proud of its burthen, swept away;
And through the lingering crowd I broke,
    Sought the hillside, and thence, heart-sick,   30
Beheld, far off, the little smoke
    Along the landscape kindling quick.

What should I do, where should I go,
    Now she was gone, my love! for mine
She was, whatever here below
    Cross'd or usurp'd my right divine.
Life, without her, was vain and gross,
    The glory from the world was gone,
And on the gardens of the Close
    As on Sahara shone the sun.   40
Oppress'd with her departed grace,
    My thoughts on ill surmises fed;

The harmful influence of the place
  She went to fill'd my soul with dread.
She, mixing with the people there,
  Might come back alter'd having caught
The foolish, fashionable air
  Of knowing all, and feeling nought.
Or, giddy with her beauty's praise,
  She'd scorn our simple country life,   50
Its wholesome nights and tranquil days,
  And would not deign to be my Wife.
'My Wife', 'my Wife', ah, tenderest word!
  How oft, as fearful she might hear,
Whispering that name of 'Wife', I heard
  The chiming of the inmost sphere.

I pass'd the home of my regret.
  The clock was striking in the hall,
And one sad window open yet,
  Although the dews began to fall.   60
Ah, distance show'd her beauty's scope!
  How light of heart and innocent
That loveliness which sicken'd hope
  And wore the world for ornament!
How perfectly her life was framed;
  And, thought of in that passionate mood,
How her affecting graces shamed
  The vulgar life that was but good!

I wonder'd, would her bird be fed,
  Her rose-plots watered, she not by;   70
Loading my breast with angry dread
  Of light, unlikely injury.

So, fill'd with love and fond remorse,
    I paced the Close, its every part
Endow'd with reliquary force
    To heal and raise from death my heart.
How tranquil and unsecular
    The precinct! Once, through yonder gate,
I saw her go, and knew from far
    Her love-lit form and gentle state.   80
Her dress had brush'd this wicket; here
    She turn'd her face, and laugh'd, with light
Like moonbeams on a wavering mere.
    Weary beforehand of the night,
I went; the blackbird, in the wood,
    Talk'd by himself, and eastward grew
In heaven the symbol of my mood,
    Where one bright star engross'd the blue.

The Prologue

Her sons pursue the butterflies,
    Her baby daughter mocks the doves
With throbbing coo; in his fond eyes
    She's Venus with her little Loves;
Her footfall dignifies the earth,
    Her form's the native-land of grace,
And, lo, his coming lights with mirth
    Its court and capital her face!
Full proud her favour makes her lord,
    And that her flatter'd bosom knows.   10
She takes his arm without a word,
    In lanes of laurel and of rose.
Ten years today has she been his.
    He but begins to understand,

He says, the dignity and bliss
    She gave him when she gave her hand
She, answering, says, he disenchants
    The past, though that was perfect; he
Rejoins, the present nothing wants
    But briefness to be ecstasy.   20
He lauds her charms; her beauty's glow
    Wins from the spoiler Time new rays;
Bright looks reply, approving so
    Beauty's elixir vitæ, praise.
Upon a beech he bids her mark
    Where, ten years since, he carved her name;
It grows there with the growing bark,
    And in his heart it grows the same.
For that her soft arm presses his
    Close to her fond, maternal breast;   30
He tells her, each new kindness is
    The effectual sum of all the rest!
And, whilst the cushat, mocking, coo'd,
    They blest the days they had been wed,
At cost of those in which he woo'd,
    Till everything was three times said;
And words were growing vain, when Briggs,
    Factotum, Footman, Butler, Groom,
Who press'd the cyder, fed the pigs,
    Preserv'd the rabbits, drove the brougham,   40
And help'd, at need, to mow the lawns,
    And sweep the paths and thatch the hay,
Here brought the Post down, Mrs Vaughan's
    Sole rival, but, for once, today,
Scarce look'd at; for the 'Second Book',
    Till this tenth festival kept close,
Was thus commenced, while o'er them shook
    The laurel married with the rose.

The Kites

I saw three Cupids (so I dream'd),
  Who made three kites, on which were drawn,
In letters that like roses gleam'd,
  'Plato', 'Anacreon', and 'Vaughan'.
The boy who held by Plato tried
  His airy venture first; all sail,
It heav'nward rush'd till scarce descried,
  Then pitch'd and dropp'd, for want of tail.
Anacreon's Love, with shouts of mirth
  That pride of spirit thus should fall,   10
To his kite link'd a lump of earth,
  And, lo, it would not soar at all.
Last, my disciple freighted his
  With a long streamer made of flowers,
The children of the sod, and this
  Rose in the sun, and flew for hours.

Lais and Lucretia

  Did first his beauty wake her sighs?
    That's Lais! Thus Lucretia's known:
  The beauty in her Lover's eyes
    Was admiration of her own.

The Kiss

'I saw you take his kiss!' ' 'Tis true.'
  'O, modesty!' ' 'Twas strictly kept:
'He thought me asleep; at least, I knew
  'He thought I thought he thought I slept.'

The Foreign Land

A woman is a foreign land,
  Of which, though there he settle young.
A man will ne'er quite understand
  The customs, politics, and tongue.
The foolish hie them post-haste through,
  See fashions odd, and prospects fair,
Learn of the language, 'How d'ye do',
  And go and brag they have been there
The most for leave to trade apply,
  For once, at Empire's seat, her heart,   10
Then get what knowledge ear and eye
  Glean chancewise in the life-long mart
And certain others, few and fit,
  Attach them to the Court, and see
The Country's best, its accent hit,
  And partly sound its polity.

Disappointment

'The bliss which woman's charms bespeak,
  'I've sought in many, found in none!'
'In many 'tis in vain you seek
  'What can be found in only one.'

The Married Lover

Why, having won her, do I woo?
  Because her spirit's vestal grace
Provokes me always to pursue,
  But, spirit-like, eludes embrace;

85

Because her womanhood is such
  That, as on court-days subjects kiss
The Queen's hand, yet so near a touch
  Affirms no mean familiarness,
Nay, rather marks more fair the height
  Which can with safety so neglect   10
To dread, as lower ladies might,
  That grace could meet with disrespect,
Thus she with happy favour feeds
  Allegiance from a love so high
That thence no false conceit proceeds
  Of difference bridged, or state put by;
Because, although in act and word
  As lowly as a wife can be,
Her manners, when they call me lord,
  Remind me 'tis by courtesy;   20
Not with her least consent of will,
  Which would my proud affection hurt,
But by the noble style that still
  Imputes an unattain'd desert;
Because her gay and lofty brows,
  When all is won which hope can ask,
Reflect a light of hopeless snows
  That bright in virgin ether bask;
Because, though free of the outer court
  I am, this Temple keeps its shrine   30
Sacred to Heaven; because, in short,
  She's not and never can be mine.

Husband and Wife

I, while the shop-girl fitted on
  The sand-shoes, look'd where, down the bay,

The sea glow'd with a shrouded sun.
  'I'm ready, Felix; will you pay?'
That was my first expense for this
  Sweet Stranger, now my three days' Wife.
How light the touches are that kiss
  The music from the chords of life!

Her feet, by half-a-mile of sea,
  In spotless sand left shapely prints;   10
With agates, then, she loaded me;
  (The lapidary call'd them flints);
Then, at her wish, I hail'd a boat,
  To take her to the ships-of-war,
At anchor, each a lazy mote
  Black in the brilliance, miles from shore.

The morning breeze the canvas fill'd,
  Lifting us o'er the bright-ridged gulf,
And every lurch my darling thrill'd
  With light fear smiling at itself;   20
And, dashing past the Arrogant,
  Asleep upon the restless wave,
After its cruise in the Levant,
  We reach'd the Wolf, and signal gave
For help to board: with caution meet,
  My bride was placed within the chair,
The red flag wrapp'd about her feet,
  And so swung laughing through the air.

'Look, Love,' she said, 'there's Frederick Graham,
  'My cousin, whom you met, you know.'   30
And seeing us, the brave man came,
  And made his frank and courteous bow,
And gave my hand a sailor's shake,
  And said, 'You ask'd me to the Hurst:

'I never thought my luck would make
   'Your wife and you my guests the first.'
And Honor, cruel, 'Nor did we:
   'Have you not lately changed your ship?'
'Yes: I'm Commander, now,' said he,
   With a slight quiver of the lip.   40
We saw the vessel, shown with pride;
   Took luncheon; I must eat his salt!
Parting he said, (I fear my bride
   Found him unselfish to a fault),
His wish, he saw, had come to pass,
   (And so, indeed, her face express'd),
That that should be, whatever 'twas,
   Which made his Cousin happiest.
We left him looking from above;
   Rich bankrupt! for he could afford   50
To say most proudly that his love
   Was virtue and its own reward.
But others loved as well as he,
   (Thought I, half-anger'd), and if fate,
Unfair, had only fashion'd me
   As hapless, I had been as great.

As souls, ambitious, but low-born,
   If raised past hope by luck or wit,
All pride of place will proudly scorn,
   And live as they'd been used to it,   60
So we two wore our strange estate:
   Familiar, unaffected, free,
We talk'd, until the dusk grew late,
   Of this and that; but, after tea,
As doubtful if a lot so sweet
   As ours was ours in very sooth,
Like children, to promote conceit,
   We feign'd that it was not the truth;

And she assumed the maiden coy,
   And I adored remorseless charms,
And then we clapp'd our hands for joy,
   And ran into each other's arms.   70

Magna Est Veritas

Here, in this little bay,
Full of tumultuous life and great repose,
Where, twice a day,
The purposeless, glad ocean comes and goes,
Under high cliffs, and far from the huge town,
I sit me down.
For want of me the world's course will not fail:
When all its work is done, the lie shall rot;
The truth is great, and shall prevail,
When none care whether it prevail or not.   10

A Farewell

With all my will, but much against my heart,
We two now part.
My Very Dear,
Our solace is, the sad road lies so clear.
It needs no art,
With faint, averted feet
And many a tear,
In our opposed paths to persevere.

Go thou to East, I West,
We will not say   10
There's any hope, it is so far away.
But, O my Best,
When the one darling of our widowhead,
The nursling Grief,
Is dead,
And no dews blur our eyes
To see the peach-bloom come in evening skies,
Perchance we may,
Where now this night is day,
And even through faith of still averted feet,   20
Making full circle of our banishment,
Amazed meet;
The bitter journey to the bourne so sweet
Seasoning the termless feast of our content
With tears of recognition never dry.

Auras of Delight

Beautiful habitations, auras of delight!
Who shall bewail the crags and bitter foam
And angry sword-blades flashing left and right
Which guard your glittering height,
That none thereby may come!
The vision which we have
Revere we so,
That yet we crave
To foot those fields of ne'er-profaned snow?
    I, with heart-quake,   10
Dreaming or thinking of that realm of Love,

See, oft, a dove
Tangled in frightful nuptials with a snake;
The tortured knot,
Now, like a kite scant-weighted, flung bewitch'd
Sunwards, now pitch'd,
Tail over head, down, but with no taste got
Eternally
Of rest in either ruin or the sky,
But bird and vermin each incessant strives,   20
With vain dilaceration of both lives,
'Gainst its abhorred bond insoluble,
Coveting fiercer any separate hell
Than the most weary soul in Purgatory
On God's sweet breast to lie.
And, in this sign, I con
The guerdon of that golden Cup, fulfill'd
With fornications foul of Babylon,
The heart where good is well-perceived and known,
Yet is not will'd;   30
And Him I thank, who can make live again
The dust, but not the joy we once profane,
That I, of ye,
Beautiful habitations, auras of delight,
In childish years and since had sometime sense and sight,
But that ye vanish'd quite,
Even from memory,
Ere I could get my breath, and whisper 'See!'
   But did for me
They altogether die,   40
Those trackless glories glimps'd in upper sky?
Were they of chance, or vain,
Nor good at all again
For curb of heart or fret?
Nay, though, by grace,
Lest, haply, I refuse God to His face,

Their likeness wholly I forget,
Ah, yet,
Often in straits which else for me were ill,
I mind me still   50
I *did* respire the lonely auras sweet,
I *did* the blest abodes behold, and, at the mountain's feet,
Bathed in the holy Stream by Hermon's thymy hill

DANTE GABRIEL ROSSETTI

My Sister's Sleep

She fell asleep on Christmas Eve:
   At length the long-ungranted shade
   Of weary eyelids overweigh'd
The pain nought else might yet relieve.

Our mother, who had leaned all day
   Over the bed from chime to chime,
   Then raised herself for the first time,
And as she sat down, did pray.

Her little work-table was spread
   With work to finish. For the glare   10
   Made by her candle, she had care
To work some distance from the bed.

Without, there was a cold moon up,
   Of winter radiance sheer and thin;
   The hollow halo it was in
Was like an icy crystal cup.

Through the small room, with subtle sound
   Of flame, by vents the fireshine drove
   And reddened. In its dim alcove
The mirror shed a clearness round.   20

I had been sitting up some nights,
   And my tired mind felt weak and blank;

93

Like a sharp strengthening wine it drank
The stillness and the broken lights.

Twelve struck. That sound, by dwindling years
  Heard in each hour, crept off; and then
  The ruffled silence spread again,
Like water that a pebble stirs.

Our mother rose from where she sat:
  Her needles, as she laid them down,   30
  Met lightly, and her silken gown
Settled: no other noise than that.

'Glory unto the Newly Born!'
  So, as said angels, she did say;
  Because we were in Christmas Day,
Though it would still be long till morn.

Just then in the room over us
There was a pushing back of chairs,
  As some who had sat unawares
So late, now heard the hour, and rose.   40

With anxious softly-stepping haste
  Our mother went where Margaret lay,
  Fearing the sounds o'erhead—should they
Have broken her long watched-for rest!

She stooped an instant, calm, and turned;
  But suddenly turned back again;
  And all her features seemed in pain
With woe, and her eyes gazed and yearned.

For my part, I but hid my face,
  And held my breath, and spoke no word: 50

There was none spoken; but I heard
The silence for a little space.

Our mother bowed herself and wept:
    And both my arms fell, and I said,
    'God knows I knew that she was dead.'
And there, all white, my sister slept.

Then kneeling, upon Christmas morn
    A little after twelve o'clock
    We said, ere the first quarter struck,
'Christ's blessing on the newly born!'   60

Lovesight

When do I see thee most, beloved one?
    When in the light the spirits of mine eyes
    Before thy face, their altar, solemnize
The worship of that Love through thee made known?
Or when in the dusk hours, (we two alone,)
    Close-kissed and eloquent of still replies
    Thy twilight-hidden glimmering visage lies,
And my soul only sees thy soul its own?

O love, my love! if I no more should see
Thyself, nor on the earth the shadow of thee,   10
    Nor image of thine eyes in any spring,—
How then should sound upon Life's darkening slope
The ground-whirl of the perished leaves of Hope,
    The wind of Death's imperishable wing?

95

Without Her

What of her glass without her? The blank grey
   There where the pool is blind of the moon's face.
   Her dress without her? The tossed empty space
Of cloud-rack whence the moon has passed away.
Her paths without her? Day's appointed sway
   Usurped by desolate night. Her pillowed place
   Without her? Tears, ah me! for love's good grace,
And cold forgetfulness of night or day.

What of the heart without her? Nay, poor heart,
   Of thee what word remains ere speech be still?   10
   A wayfarer by barren ways and chill,
Steep ways and weary, without her thou art,
Where the long cloud, the long wood's counterpart,
   Sheds doubled darkness up the labouring hill.

Sudden Light

I have been here before,
   But when or how I cannot tell:
I know the grass beyond the door,
   The sweet keen smell,
The sighing sound, the lights around the shore.

You have been mine before,—
   How long ago I may not know:
But just when at that swallow's soar
   Your neck turned so,
Some veil did fall,—I knew it all of yore.   10

96

[handwritten: Then now, or then and now]

Then, now,—perchance again! ...
    O round mine eyes your tresses shake! *[handwritten: lying down]*
Shall we not lie as we have lain
    Thus for Love's sake,
And sleep, and wake, yet never break the chain?

[handwritten: act & simply implied — transcendence of love found in ? 1881 version; also less ambiguous]

[handwritten: earlier stanza, 1863-1870 editions, 'Song IV' in Songs towards a work to be called 'the House of Life']

The Woodspurge

The wind flapped loose, the wind was still,
Shaken out dead from tree and hill:
I had walked on at the wind's will,—
I sat now, for the wind was still.

Between my knees my forehead was,—
My lips, drawn in, said not Alas!
My hair was over in the grass,
My naked ears heard the day pass.

My eyes, wide open, had the run
Of some ten weeds to fix upon;   10
Among those few, out of the sun,
The woodspurge flowered, three cups in one.

From perfect grief there need not be
Wisdom or even memory:
One thing then learnt remains to me,—
The woodspurge has a cup of three.

The Honeysuckle

I plucked a honeysuckle where
  The hedge on high is quick with thorn,
  And climbing for the prize, was torn,
And fouled my feet in quag-water;
  And by the thorns and by the wind
  The blossom that I took was thinn'd,
And yet I found it sweet and fair.

Thence to a richer growth I came,
  Where, nursed in mellow intercourse,
  The honeysuckles sprang by scores,   10
Not harried like my single stem,
  All virgin lamps of scent and dew.
  So from my hand that first I threw,
Yet plucked not any more of them.

Even So

    So it is, my dear.
All such things touch secret strings
    For heavy hearts to hear.
    So it is, my dear.

    Very like indeed:
Sea and sky, afar, on high,
    Sand and strewn seaweed,—
    Very like indeed.

But the sea stands spread
As one wall with the flat skies,   10
Where the lean black craft like flies
  Seem well-nigh stagnated,
  Soon to drop off dead.

Seemed it so to us
When I was thine and thou wast mine,
  And all these things were thus,
  But all our world in us?

Could we be so now?
Not if all beneath heaven's pall
  Lay dead but I and thou,   20
  Could we be so now!

The Mirror

She knew it not:—most perfect pain
  To learn: this too she knew not. Strife
    For me, calm hers, as from the first.
    'Twas but another bubble burst
  Upon the curdling draught of life,—
My silent patience mine again.

As who, of forms that crowd unknown
  Within a distant mirror's shade,
    Deems such an one himself, and makes
    Some sign; but when the image shakes   10
  No whit, he finds his thought betray'd,
And must seek elsewhere for his own.

99

The Orchard-Pit

Piled deep below the screening orchard-branch
  They lie with bitter apples in their hands:
And some are only ancient bones that blanch,
And some had ships that last year's wind did launch,
  And some were yesterday the lords of lands.

In the soft dell, among the apple-trees,
  High up above the hidden pit she stands,
And there for ever sings, who gave to these,
That lie below, her magic hour of ease,
  And those her apples holden in their hands.   10

This in my dreams is shown me; and her hair
  Crosses my lips and draws my burning breath;
Her song spreads golden wings upon the air,
Life's eyes are gleaming from her forehead fair,
  And from her breasts the ravishing eyes of Death.

Men say to me that sleep hath many dreams,
  Yet I knew never but this dream alone:
There, from a dried-up channel, once the stream's,
The glen slopes up; even such in sleep it seems
  As to my walking sight the place well known.   20

      *   *   *   *   *

My love I call her, and she loves me well:
  But I love her as in the maelstrom's cup
The whirled stone loves the leaf inseparable
That clings to it round all the circling swell,
  And that the same last eddy swallows up.

CHRISTINA ROSSETTI

Goblin Market

Morning and evening
Maids heard the goblins cry:
'Come buy our orchard fruits,
Come buy, come buy:
Apples and quinces,
Lemons and oranges,
Plump unpecked cherries,
Melons and raspberries,
Bloom-down-cheeked peaches,
Swart-headed mulberries,   10
Wild free-born cranberries,
Crab-apples, dewberries,
Pine-apples, blackberries,
Apricots, strawberries;—
All ripe together
In summer weather,—
Morns that pass by,
Fair eves that fly;
Come buy, come buy:
Our grapes fresh from the vine,   20
Pomegranates full and fine,
Dates and sharp bullaces,
Rare pears and greengages,
Damsons and bilberries,
Taste them and try:
Currants and gooseberries,
Bright-fire-like barberries,

Figs to fill your mouth,
Citrons from the South,
Sweet to tongue and sound to eye;   30
Come buy, come buy.'

   Evening by evening
Among the brookside rushes,
Laura bowed her head to hear,
Lizzie veiled her blushes:
Crouching close together
In the cooling weather,
With clasping arms and cautioning lips,
With tingling cheeks and finger tips.
'Lie close,' Laura said,   40
Pricking up her golden head:
'We must not look at goblin men,
We must not buy their fruits:
Who knows upon what soil they fed
Their hungry thirsty roots?'
'Come buy,' call the goblins
Hobbling down the glen.
'Oh,' cried Lizzie, 'Laura, Laura,
You should not peep at goblin men.'
Lizzie covered up her eyes,   50
Covered close lest they should look;
Laura reared her glossy head,
And whispered like the restless brook:
'Look, Lizzie, look, Lizzie,
Down the glen tramp little men.
One hauls a basket,
One bears a plate,
One lugs a golden dish
Of many pounds weight.
How fair the vine must grow   60
Whose grapes are so luscious;

How warm the wind must blow
Through those fruit bushes.'
'No,' said Lizzie: 'No, no, no;
Their offers should not charm us,
Their evil gifts would harm us.'
She thrust a dimpled finger
In each ear, shut eyes and ran:
Curious Laura chose to linger
Wondering at each merchant man.   70
One had a cat's face,
One whisked a tail,
One tramped at a rat's pace,
One crawled like a snail,
One like a wombat prowled obtuse and furry,
One like a ratel tumbled hurry skurry.
She heard a voice like voice of doves
Cooing all together:
They sounded kind and full of loves
In the pleasant weather.   80

    Laura stretched her gleaming neck
Like a rush-imbedded swan,
Like a lily from the beck,
Like a moonlit poplar branch,
Like a vessel at the launch
When its last restraint is gone.

    Backwards up the mossy glen
Turned and trooped the goblin men,
With their shrill repeated cry,
'Come buy, come buy.'   90
When they reached where Laura was
They stood stock still upon the moss,
Leering at each other,
Brother with queer brother;

Signalling each other,
Brother with sly brother.
One set his basket down,
One reared his plate;
One began to weave a crown
Of tendrils, leaves, and rough nuts brown 100
(Men sell not such in any town);
One heaved the golden weight
Of dish and fruit to offer her:
'Come buy, come buy,' was still their cry.
Laura stared but did not stir,
Longed but had no money:
The whisk-tailed merchant bade her taste
In tones as smooth as honey,
The cat-faced purr'd,
The rat-paced spoke a word 110
Of welcome, and the snail-paced even was heard;
One parrot-voiced and jolly
Cried 'Pretty Goblin' still for 'Pretty Polly;'—
One whistled like a bird.

But sweet-tooth Laura spoke in haste:
'Good folk, I have no coin;
To take were to purloin:
I have no copper in my purse,
I have no silver either,
And all my gold is on the furze 120
That shakes in windy weather
Above the rusty heather.'
'You have much gold upon your head,'
They answered all together:
'Buy from us with a golden curl.'
She clipped a precious golden lock,
She dropped a tear more rare than pearl,
Then sucked their fruit globes fair or red:

Sweeter than honey from the rock,
Stronger than man-rejoicing wine,   130
Clearer than water flowed that juice;
She never tasted such before,
How should it cloy with length of use?
She sucked and sucked and sucked the more
Fruits which that unknown orchard bore;
She sucked until her lips were sore;
Then flung the emptied rinds away
But gathered up one kernel stone,
And knew not was it night or day
As she turned home alone.   140

   Lizzie met her at the gate
Full of wise upbraidings:
'Dear, you should not stay so late,
Twilight is not good for maidens;
Should not loiter in the glen
In the haunts of goblin men.
Do you not remember Jeanie,
How she met them in the moonlight,
Took their gifts both choice and many,
Ate their fruits and wore their flowers   150
Plucked from bowers
Where summer ripens at all hours?
But ever in the noonlight
She pined and pined away;
Sought them by night and day,
Found them no more but dwindled and grew grey;
Then fell with the first snow,
While to this day no grass will grow
Where she lies low:
I planted daisies there a year ago   160
That never blow.
You should not loiter so.'

'Nay, hush,' said Laura:
'Nay, hush, my sister:
I ate and ate my fill,
Yet my mouth waters still;
Tomorrow night I will
Buy more:' and kissed her:
'Have done with sorrow;
I'll bring you plums tomorrow   170
Fresh on their mother twigs,
Cherries worth getting;
You cannot think what figs
My teeth have met in,
What melons icy-cold
Piled on a dish of gold
Too huge for me to hold,
What peaches with a velvet nap,
Pellucid grapes without one seed:
Odorous indeed must be the mead   180
Wheron they grow, and pure the wave they drink
With lilies at the brink,
And sugar-sweet their sap.'

  Golden head by golden head,
Like two pigeons in one nest
Folded in each other's wings,
They lay down in their curtained bed:
Like two blossoms on one stem,
Like two flakes of new-fall'n snow,
Like two wands of ivory   190
Tipped with gold for awful kings.
Moon and stars gazed in at them,
Wind sang to them lullaby,
Lumbering owls forbore to fly,
Not a bat flapped to and fro
Round their nest:

Cheek to cheek and breast to breast
Locked together in one nest.

Early in the morning
When the first cock crowed his warning,   200
Neat like bees, as sweet and busy,
Laura rose with Lizzie:
Fetched in honey, milked the cows,
Aired and set to rights the house,
Kneaded cakes of whitest wheat,
Cakes for dainty mouths to eat,
Next churned butter, whipped up cream,
Fed their poultry, sat and sewed;
Talked as modest maidens should:
Lizzie with an open heart,   210
Laura in an absent dream,
One content, one sick in part;
One warbling for the mere bright day's delight,
One longing for the night.

At length slow evening came:
They went with pitchers to the reedy brook;
Lizzie most placid in her look,
Laura most like a leaping flame.
They drew the gurgling water from its deep;
Lizzie plucked purple and rich golden flags,   220
Then turning homewards said: 'The sunset flushes
Those furthest loftiest crags;
Come, Laura, not another maiden lags,
No wilful squirrel wags,
The beasts and birds are fast asleep.'
But Laura loitered still among the rushes
And said the bank was steep.

And said the hour was early still,
The dew not fall'n, the wind not chill:

Listening ever, but not catching
The customary cry,
'Come buy, come buy,'
With its iterated jingle
Of sugar-baited words:
Not for all her watching
Once discerning even one goblin
Racing, whisking, tumbling, hobbling;
Let alone the herds
That used to tramp along the glen,
In groups or single, 240
Of brisk fruit-merchant men.

Till Lizzie urged, 'O Laura, come;
I hear the fruit-call but I dare not look:
You should not loiter longer at this brook:
Come with me home.
The stars rise, the moon bends her arc,
Each glowworm winks her spark,
Let us get home before the night grows dark:
For clouds may gather
Though this is summer weather, 250
Put out the lights and drench us through;
Then if we lost our way what should we do?'

Laura turned cold as stone
To find her sister heard that cry alone,
That goblin cry,
'Come buy our fruits, come buy.'
Must she then buy no more such dainty fruit?
Must she no more such succous pasture find,
Gone deaf and blind?
Her tree of life drooped from the root: 260
She said not one word in her heart's sore ache;
But peering thro' the dimness, nought discerning,

Trudged home, her pitcher dripping all the way;
So crept to bed, and lay
Silent till Lizzie slept;
Then sat up in a passionate yearning,
And gnashed her teeth for baulked desire, and wept
As if her heart would break.

    Day after day, night after night,
Laura kept watch in vain   270
In sullen silence of exceeding pain.
She never caught again the goblin cry:
'Come buy, come buy;'—
She never spied the goblin men
Hawking their fruits along the glen:
But when the noon waxed bright
Her hair grew thin and grey;
She dwindled, as the fair full moon doth turn
To swift decay and burn
Her fire away.   280

    One day remembering her kernel stone
She set it by a wall that faced the south;
Dewed it with tears, hoped for a root,
Watched for a waxing shoot,
But there came none;
It never saw the sun,
It never felt the trickling moisture run:
While with sunk eyes and faded mouth
She dreamed of melons, as a traveller sees
False waves in desert drouth   290
With shade of leaf-crowned trees,
And burns the thirstier in the sandful breeze.

    She no more swept the house,
Tended the fowls or cows,
Fetched honey, kneaded cakes of wheat,

109

Brought water from the brook:
But sat down listless in the chimney-nook
And would not eat.

   Tender Lizzie could not bear
To watch her sister's cankerous care   300
Yet not to share.
She night and morning
Caught the goblins' cry:
'Come buy our orchard fruits,
Come buy, come buy:'—
Beside the brook, along the glen,
She heard the tramp of goblin men,
The voice and stir
Poor Laura could not hear;
Longed to buy fruit to comfort her,   310
But feared to pay too dear.
She thought of Jeanie in her grave,
Who should have been a bride;
But who for joys brides hope to have
Fell sick and died
In her gay prime,
In earliest Winter time,
With the first glazing rime,
With the first snow-fall of crisp Winter time.

   Till Laura dwindling   320
Seemed knocking at Death's door:
Then Lizzie weighed no more
Better and worse;
But put a silver penny in her purse,
Kissed Laura, crossed the heath with clumps of furze
At twilight, halted by the brook:
And for the first time in her life
Began to listen and look.

Laughed every goblin
When they spied her peeping: 330
Came towards her hobbling,
Flying, running, leaping,
Puffing and blowing,
Chuckling, clapping, crowing,
Clucking and gobbling,
Mopping and mowing,
Full of airs and graces,
Pulling wry faces,
Demure grimaces,
Cat-like and rat-like, 340
Ratel- and wombat-like,
Snail-paced in a hurry,
Parrot-voiced and whistler,
Helter skelter, hurry skurry,
Chattering like magpies,
Fluttering like pigeons,
Gliding like fishes,—
Hugged her and kissed her:
Squeezed and caressed her:
Stretched up their dishes, 350
Panniers, and plates:
'Look at our apples
Russet and dun,
Bob at our cherries,
Bite at our peaches,
Citrons and dates,
Grapes for the asking,
Pears red with basking
Out in the sun,
Plums on their twigs; 360
Pluck them and suck them,
Pomegranates, figs.'—

'Good folk,' said Lizzie,
Mindful of Jeanie:
'Give me much and many:'—
Held out her apron,
Tossed them her penny.
'Nay, take a seat with us,
Honour and eat with us,'
They answered grinning:
'Our feast is but beginning.
Night yet is early,
Warm and dew-pearly,
Wakeful and starry:
Such fruits as these
No man can carry;
Half their bloom would fly,
Half their dew would dry,
Half their flavour would pass by.
Sit down and feast with us,
Be welcome guest with us,
Cheer you and rest with us.'—
'Thank you,' said Lizzie: 'But one waits
At home alone for me:
So without further parleying,
If you will not sell me any
Of your fruits though much and many,
Give me back my silver penny
I tossed you for a fee.'—
They began to scratch their pates,
No longer wagging, purring,
But visibly demurring,
Grunting and snarling.
One called her proud,
Cross-grained, uncivil;
Their tones waxed loud,
Their looks were evil.

370

380

390

Lashing their tails
They trod and hustled her,
Elbowed and jostled her,   400
Clawed with their nails,
Barking, mewing, hissing, mocking,
Tore her gown and soiled her stocking,
Twitched her hair out by the roots,
Stamped upon her tender feet,
Held her hands and squeezed their fruits
Against her mouth to make her eat.

    White and golden Lizzie stood,
Like a lily in a flood,—
Like a rock of blue-veined stone   410
Lashed by tides obstreperously,—
Like a beacon left alone
In a hoary roaring sea,
Sending up a golden fire,—
Like a fruit-crowned orange-tree
White with blossoms honey-sweet
Sore beset by wasp and bee,—
Like a royal virgin town
Topped with gilded dome and spire
Close beleaguered by a fleet   420
Mad to tug her standard down.

    One may lead a horse to water,
Twenty cannot make him drink.
Though the goblins cuffed and caught her,
Coaxed and fought her,
Bullied and besought her,
Scratched her, pinched her black as ink,
Kicked and knocked her,
Mauled and mocked her,

Lizzie uttered not a word; 430
Would not open lip from lip
Lest they should cram a mouthful in:
But laughed in heart to feel the drip
Of juice that syrupped all her face,
And lodged in dimples of her chin,
And streaked her neck which quaked like curd.
At last the evil people
Worn out by her resistance
Flung back her penny, kicked their fruit
Along whichever road they took, 440
Not leaving root or stone or shoot;
Some writhed into the ground,
Some dived into the brook
With ring and ripple,
Some scudded on the gale without a sound,
Some vanished in the distance.

    In a smart, ache, tingle,
Lizzie went her way;
Knew not was it night or day;
Sprang up the bank, tore thro' the furze, 450
Threaded copse and dingle,
And heard her penny jingle
Bouncing in her purse,—
Its bounce was music to her ear.
She ran and ran
As if she feared some goblin man
Dogged her with gibe or curse
Or something worse:
But not one goblin scurried after,
Nor was she pricked by fear; 460
The kind heart made her windy-paced
That urged her home quite out of breath with haste
And inward laughter.

She cried 'Laura,' up the garden,
'Did you miss me?
Come and kiss me.
Never mind my bruises,
Hug me, kiss me, suck my juices
Squeezed from goblin fruits for you,
Goblin pulp and goblin dew.   470
Eat me, drink me, love me;
Laura, make much of me:
For your sake I have braved the glen
And had to do with goblin merchant men.'

Laura started from her chair,
Flung her arms up in the air,
Clutched her hair:
'Lizzie, Lizzie, have you tasted
For my sake the fruit forbidden?
Must your light like mine be hidden,   480
Your young life like mine be wasted,
Undone in mine undoing
And ruined in my ruin,
Thirsty, cankered, goblin-ridden?'—
She clung about her sister,
Kissed and kissed and kissed her:
Tears once again
Refreshed her shrunken eyes,
Dropping like rain
After long sultry drouth;   490
Shaking with aguish fear, and pain,
She kissed and kissed her with a hungry mouth.

Her lips began to scorch,
That juice was wormwood to her tongue,
She loathed the feast:
Writhing as one possessed she leaped and sung,

Rent all her robe, and wrung
Her hands in lamentable haste,
And beat her breast.
Her locks streamed like the torch   500
Borne by a racer at full speed,
Or like the mane of horses in their flight,
Or like an eagle when she stems the light
Straight towards the sun,
Or like a caged thing freed,
Or like a flying flag when armies run.

   Swift fire spread through her veins, knocked at her heart,
Met the fire smouldering there
And overbore its lesser flame;
She gorged on bitterness without a name: 510
Ah! fool, to choose such part
Of soul-consuming care!
Sense failed in the mortal strife:
Like the watch-tower of a town
Which an earthquake shatters down,
Like a lightning-stricken mast,
Like a wind-uprooted tree
Spun about,
Like a foam-topped waterspout
Cast down headlong in the sea,   520
She fell at last;
Pleasure past and anguish past,
Is it death or is it life?

   Life out of death.
That night long Lizzie watched by her,
Counted her pulse's flagging stir,
Felt for her breath,
Held water to her lips, and cooled her face
With tears and fanning leaves:

116

But when the first birds chirped about their eaves,
And early reapers plodded to the place   530
Of golden sheaves,
And dew-wet grass
Bowed in the morning winds so brisk to pass,
And new buds with new day
Opened of cup-like lilies on the stream,
Laura awoke as from a dream,
Laughed in the innocent old way,
Hugged Lizzie but not twice or thrice;
Her gleaming locks showed not one thread of grey,
Her breath was sweet as May   540
And light danced in her eyes.

   Days, weeks, months, years
Afterwards, when both were wives
With children of their own;
Their mother-hearts beset with fears,
Their lives bound up in tender lives;
Laura would call the little ones
And tell them of her early prime,
Those pleasant days long gone   550
Of not-returning time:
Would talk about the haunted glen,
The wicked, quaint fruit-merchant men,
Their fruits like honey to the throat
But poison in the blood;
(Men sell not such in any town:)
Would tell them how her sister stood
In deadly peril to do her good,
And win the fiery antidote:
Then joining hands to little hands   560
Would bid them cling together,
'For there is no friend like a sister
In calm or stormy weather;

117

To cheer one on the tedious way,
To fetch one if one goes astray,
To lift one if one totters down,
To strengthen whilst one stands.'

The Three Enemies

The Flesh

'Sweet, thou art pale.'
                                    'More pale to see,
Christ hung upon the cruel tree
And bore His Father's wrath for me.'

'Sweet, thou art sad.'
                                    'Beneath a rod
More heavy, Christ for my sake trod
The winepress of the wrath of God.'

'Sweet, thou art weary.'
                                    'Not so Christ:
Whose mighty love of me sufficed
For Strength, Salvation, Eucharist.'

'Sweet, thou art footsore.'
                                    'If I bleed,   10
His feet have bled: yea, in my need
His Heart once bled for mine indeed.'

The World

'Sweet, thou art young.'
                              'So He was young
Who for my sake in silence hung
Upon the Cross with Passion wrung.'

'Look, thou art fair.'
                              'He was more fair
Than men, Who deigned for me to wear
A visage marred beyond compare.'

'And thou hast riches.'
                              'Daily bread:
All else is His; Who living, dead,   20
For me lacked where to lay His Head.'

'And life is sweet.'
                              'It was not so
To Him, Whose Cup did overflow
With mine unutterable woe.'

The Devil

'Thou drinkest deep.'
                              'When Christ would sup
He drained the dregs from out my cup:
So how should I be lifted up?'

'Thou shalt win Glory.'
                              'In the skies,
Lord Jesus, cover up mine eyes
Lest they should look on vanities.'   30

'Thou shalt have Knowledge.'
'Helpless dust!
In Thee, O Lord, I put my trust:
Answer Thou for me, Wise and Just.'

'And Might.'—
'Get thee behind me. Lord,
Who hast redeemed and not abhorred
My soul, oh keep it by Thy Word.'

From

The Prince's Progress

Too late for love, too late for joy,
   Too late, too late!
You loitered on the road too long,
   You trifled at the gate:
The enchanted dove upon her branch
   Died without a mate;
The enchanted princess in her tower
   Slept, died, behind the grate;
Her heart was starving all this while
   You made it wait.   10

Ten years ago, five years ago,
   One year ago,
Even then you had arrived in time,
   Though somewhat slow;
Then you had known her living face
   Which now you cannot know:
The frozen fountain would have leaped,
   The buds gone on to blow,
The warm south wind would have awaked
   To melt the snow.   20

Is she fair now as she lies?
  Once she was fair;
Meet queen for any kingly king,
  With gold-dust on her hair.
Now these are poppies in her locks,
  White poppies she must wear;
Must wear a veil to shroud her face
  And the want graven there:
Or is the hunger fed at length,
  Cast off the care?   30

We never saw her with a smile
  Or with a frown;
Her bed seemed never soft to her,
  Though tossed of down;
She little heeded what she wore,
  Kirtle, or wreath, or gown;
We think her white brows often ached
  Beneath her crown,
Till silvery hairs showed in her locks
  That used to be so brown.   40

We never heard her speak in haste:
  Her tones were sweet,
And modulated just so much
  As it was meet:
Her heart sat silent through the noise
  And concourse of the street.
There was no hurry in her hands,
  No hurry in her feet;
There was no bliss drew nigh to her,
  That she might run to greet.   50

You should have wept her yesterday,
  Wasting upon her bed:

But wherefore should you weep today
  That she is dead?
Lo, we who love weep not today,
  But crown her royal head.
Let be these poppies that we strew,
  Your roses are too red:
Let be these poppies, not for you
  Cut down and spread.   60

The Queen of Hearts

How comes it, Flora, that, whenever we
Play cards together, you invariably,
  However the pack parts,
  Still hold the Queen of Hearts?

I've scanned you with a scrutinizing gaze,
Resolved to fathom these your secret ways:
  But, sift them as I will,
  Your ways are secret still.

I cut and shuffle; shuffle, cut, again;
But all my cutting, shuffling, proves in vain: 10
  Vain hope, vain forethought too;
  That Queen still falls to you.

I dropped her once, prepense; but, ere the deal
Was dealt, your instinct seemed her loss to feel:
  'There should be one card more,'
  You said, and searched the floor.

I cheated once; I made a private notch
In Heart-Queen's back, and kept a lynx-eyed watch;
  Yet such another back
  Deceived me in the pack: 20

122

The Queen of Clubs assumed by arts unknown
An imitative dint that seemed my own;
    This notch, not of my doing,
    Misled me to my ruin.

It baffles me to puzzle out the clue,
Which must be skill, or craft, or luck in you:
    Unless, indeed, it be
    Natural affinity.

Memory

I

I nursed it in my bosom while it lived,
  I hid it in my heart when it was dead;
In joy I sat alone, even so I grieved
    Alone and nothing said.

I shut the door to face the naked truth,
  I stood alone—I faced the truth alone,
Stripped bare of self-regard or forms or ruth
    Till first and last were shown.

I took the perfect balances and weighed;
  No shaking of my hand disturbed the poise;   10
Weighed, found it wanting: not a word I said,
    But silent made my choice.

None know the choice I made; I make it still.
  None know the choice I made and broke my heart,
Breaking mine idol: I have braced my will
    Once, chosen for once my part.

I broke it at a blow, I laid it cold,
  Crushed in my deep heart where it used to live.

My heart dies inch by inch; the time grows old,
   Grows old in which I grieve.

2

I have a room whereinto no one enters
   Save I myself alone:
   There sits a blessed memory on a throne,
There my life centres.

While winter comes and goes—oh tedious comer!—
   And while its nip-wind blows;
   While bloom the bloodless lily and warm rose
Of lavish summer.

If any should force entrance he might see there
   One buried yet not dead,
   Before whose face I no more bow my head
Or bend my knee there;

But often in my worn life's autumn weather
   I watch there with clear eyes,
   And think how it will be in Paradise
When we're together.

Eve

'While I sit at the door
Sick to gaze within
Mine eye weepeth sore
For sorrow and sin:
As a tree my sin stands
To darken all lands;
Death is the fruit it bore.

'How have Eden bowers grown
Without Adam to bend them!
How have Eden flowers blown   10
Squandering their sweet breath
Without me to tend them!
The Tree of Life was ours,
Tree twelvefold-fruited,
Most lofty tree that flowers,
Most deeply rooted:
I chose the tree of death.

'Hadst thou but said me nay,
Adam, my brother,
I might have pined away;   20
I, but none other:
God might have let thee stay
Safe in our garden,
By putting me away
Beyond all pardon.

'I, Eve, sad mother
Of all who must live,
I, not another
Plucked bitterest fruit to give
My friend, husband, lover   30
O wanton eyes run over;
Who but I should grieve?—
Cain hath slain his brother:
Of all who must die mother,
Miserable Eve!'

Thus she sat weeping,
Thus Eve our mother,
Where one lay sleeping
Slain by his brother.

Greatest and least   40
Each piteous beast
To hear her voice
Forgot his joys
And set aside his feast.

The mouse paused in his walk
And dropped his wheaten stalk;
Grave cattle wagged their heads
In rumination;
The eagle gave a cry
From his cloud station;   50
Larks on thyme beds
Forbore to mount or sing;
Bees drooped upon the wing;
The raven perched on high
Forgot his ration;
The conies in their rock,
A feeble nation,
Quaked sympathetical;
The mocking-bird left off to mock;
Huge camels knelt as if   60
In deprecation;
The kind hart's tears were falling;
Chattered the wistful stork;
Dove-voices with a dying fall
Cooed desolation
Answering grief by grief.

Only the serpent in the dust
Wriggling and crawling
Grinned an evil grin and thrust
His tongue out with its fork.   70

ALGERNON CHARLES SWINBURNE

Choruses from

Atalanta in Calydon

When the hounds of spring

When the hounds of spring are on winter's traces,
   The mother of months in meadow or plain
Fills the shadows and windy places
   With lisp of leaves and ripple of rain;
And the brown bright nightingale amorous
Is half assuaged for Itylus,
For the Thracian ships and the foreign faces,
   The tongueless vigil, and all the pain.

Come with bows bent and with emptying of quivers,
   Maiden most perfect, lady of light,   10
With a noise of winds and many rivers,
   With a clamour of waters, and with might;
Bind on thy sandals, O thou most fleet,
Over the splendour and speed of thy feet;
For the faint east quickens, the wan west shivers,
   Round the feet of the day and the feet of the night.

Where shall we find her, how shall we sing to her,
   Fold our hands round her knees, and cling?
O that man's heart were as fire and could spring to her,
   Fire, or the strength of the streams that spring!   20

For the stars and the winds are unto her
As raiment, as songs of the harp-player;
For the risen stars and the fallen cling to her,
    And the southwest-wind and the west-wind sing.

For winter's rains and ruins are over,
    And all the season of snows and sins;
The days dividing lover and lover,
    The light that loses, the night that wins;
And time remembered is grief forgotten,
And frosts are slain and flowers begotten,   30
And in green underwood and cover
    Blossom by blossom the spring begins.

The full streams feed on flower of rushes,
    Ripe grasses trammel a travelling foot,
The faint fresh flame of the young year flushes
    From leaf to flower and flower to fruit;
And fruit and leaf are as gold and fire,
And the oat is heard above the lyre,
And the hoofèd heel of a satyr crushes
    The chestnut-husk at the chestnut-root.   40

And Pan by noon and Bacchus by night,
    Fleeter of foot than the fleet-foot kid,
Follows with dancing and fills with delight
    The Maenad and the Bassarid;
And soft as lips that laugh and hide
The laughing leaves of the trees divide,
And screen from seeing and leave in sight
    The god pursuing, the maiden hid.

The ivy falls with the Bacchanal's hair
    Over her eyebrows hiding her eyes;   50
The wild vine slipping down leaves bare
    Her bright breast shortening into sighs;

The wild vine slips with the weight of its leaves,
But the berried ivy catches and cleaves
To the limbs that glitter, the feet that scare
    The wolf that follows, the fawn that flies.

Before the beginning of years

    Before the beginning of years
        There came to the making of man
    Time, with a gift of tears;
        Grief, with a glass that ran;
    Pleasure, with pain for leaven;
        Summer, with flowers that fell;
    Remembrance fallen from heaven,
        And madness risen from hell;
    Strength without hands to smite;
        Love that endures for a breath: 10
    Night, the shadow of light,
        And life, the shadow of death.

    And the high gods took in hand
        Fire, and the falling of tears,
    And a measure of sliding sand
        From under the feet of the years;
    And froth and drift of the sea;
        And dust of the labouring earth;
    And bodies of things to be
        In the houses of death and of birth;   20
    And wrought with weeping and laughter,
        And fashioned with loathing and love,
    With life before and after
        And death beneath and above,
    For a day and a night and a morrow,
        That his strength might endure for a span

With travail and heavy sorrow,
   The holy spirit of man.

From the winds of the north and the south
   They gathered as unto strife;   30
They breathed upon his mouth,
   They filled his body with life;
Eyesight and speech they wrought
   For the veils of the soul therein,
A time for labour and thought,
   A time to serve and to sin;
They gave him light in his ways,
   And love, and a space for delight,
And beauty and length of days,
   And night, and sleep in the night.   40
His speech is a burning fire;
   With his lips he travaileth;
In his heart is a blind desire,
   In his eyes foreknowledge of death;
He weaves, and is clothed with derision;
   Sows, and he shall not reap;
His life is a watch or a vision
   Between a sleep and a sleep.

Let your hands meet

MELEAGER

Let your hands meet
   Round the weight of my head;
Lift ye my feet
   As the feet of the dead;
For the flesh of my body is molten, the limbs of it molten as lead.

O thy luminous face,
    Thine imperious eyes!
O the grief, O the grace,
    As of day when it dies!
Who is this bending over thee, lord, with tears and suppression of
  sighs?   10

MELEAGER
Is a bride so fair?
    Is a maid so meek?
With unchapleted hair,
    With unfilleted cheek,
Atalanta, the pure among women, whose name is as blessing to speak.

ATALANTA
I would that with feet
    Unsandalled, unshod,
Overbold, overfleet,
    I had swum not nor trod
From Arcadia to Calydon northward, a blast of the envy of God. 20

MELEAGER
Unto each man his fate;
    Unto each as he saith
In whose fingers the weight
    Of the world is as breath;
Yet I would that in clamour of battle mine hands had laid hold
  upon death.

CHORUS
Not with cleaving of shields
    And their clash in thine ear,

When the lord of fought fields
    Breaketh spearshaft from spear,
Thou art broken, our lord, thou art broken, with travail and labour
    and fear.   30

Would God he had found me
    Beneath fresh boughs!
Would God he had bound me
    Unawares in mine house,
With light in mine eyes, and songs in my lips, and a crown on my
    brows!

Whence art thou sent from us?
    Whither thy goal?
How art thou rent from us,
    Thou that wert whole,
As with severing of eyelids and eyes, as with sundering of body
    and soul!   40

My heart is within me
    As an ash in the fire;
Whosoever hath seen me,
    Without lute, without lyre,
Shall sing of me grievous things, even things that were ill to desire.

Who shall raise thee
    From the house of the dead?
Or what man praise thee
    That thy praise may be said?
Alas thy beauty! alas thy body! alas thine head!   50

But thou, O mother,
The dreamer of dreams,
Wilt thou bring forth another
To feel the sun's beams
When I move among shadows a shadow, and wail by impassable
streams?

OENEUS

What thing wilt thou leave me
Now this thing is done?
A man wilt thou give me,
A son for my son,
For the light of mine eyes, the desire of my life, the desirable one? 60

CHORUS

Thou wert glad above others,
Yea, fair beyond word;
Thou wert glad among mothers;
For each man that heard
Of thee, praise there was added unto thee, as wings to the feet of
a bird.

OENEUS

Who shall give back
Thy face of old years,
With travail made black,
Grown grey among fears,
Mother of sorrow, mother of cursing, mother of tears?   70

MELEAGER

Though thou art as fire
Fed with fuel in vain,

133

My delight, my desire,
  Is more chaste than the rain,
More pure than the dewfall, more holy than stars are that live
  without stain.

ATALANTA

I would that as water
  My life's blood had thawn,
Or as winter's wan daughter
  Leaves lowland and lawn
Spring-stricken, or ever mine eyes had beheld thee made dark in
  thy dawn.   80

CHORUS

When thou dravest the men
  Of the chosen of Thrace,
None turned him again
  Nor endured he thy face
Clothed round with the blush of the battle, with light from a
  terrible place.

OENEUS

Thou shouldst die as he dies
  For whom none sheddeth tears;
Filling thine eyes
  And fulfilling thine ears
With the brilliance of battle, the bloom and the beauty, the
  splendour of spears.   90

CHORUS

In the ears of the world
  It is sung, it is told,
And the light thereof hurled
  And the noise thereof rolled
From the Acroceraunian snow to the ford of the fleece of gold.

Would God ye could carry me
Forth of all these;
Heap sand and bury me
By the Chersonese
Where the thundering Bosphorus answers the thunder of Pontic
seas.   100

OENEUS
Dost thou mock at our praise
And the singing begun
And the men of strange days
Praising my son
In the folds of the hills of home, high places of Calydon?

MELEAGER
For the dead man no home is;
Ah, better to be
What the flower of the foam is
In fields of the sea,
That the sea-waves might be as my raiment, the gulf-stream a
garment for me.   110

CHORUS
Who shall seek thee and bring
And restore thee thy day,
When the dove dipt her wing
And the oars won their way
Where the narrowing Symplegades whitened the straits of
Propontis with spray?

MELEAGER
Will ye crown me my tomb
Or exalt me my name,

135

Now my spirits consume,
Now my flesh is a flame?
Let the sea slake it once, and men speak of me sleeping to praise
me or shame.   120

Turn back now, turn thee,
As who turns him to wake;
Though the life in thee burn thee,
Couldst thou bathe it and slake
Where the sea-ridge of Helle hangs heavier, and east upon west
waters break?

Would the winds blow me back
Or the waves hurl me home?
Ah, to touch in the track
Where the pine learnt to roam
Cold girdles and crowns of the sea-gods, cool blossoms of water
and foam!   130

The gods may release
That they made fast;
Thy soul shall have ease
In thy limbs at the last;
But what shall they give thee for life, sweet life that is overpast?

Not the life of men's veins,
Not of flesh that conceives;
But the grace that remains,
The fair beauty that cleaves
To the life of the rains in the grasses, the life of the dews on the
leaves.   140

CHORUS

Thou wert helmsman and chief;
Wilt thou turn in an hour,
Thy limbs to the leaf,
Thy face to the flower,
Thy blood to the water, thy soul to the gods who divide and
devour?

MELEAGER

The years are hungry,
They wail all their days;
The gods wax angry
And weary of praise;
And who shall bridle their lips? and who shall straiten their
ways?   150

CHORUS

The gods guard over us
With sword and with rod;
Weaving shadow to cover us,
Heaping the sod,
That law may fulfil herself wholly, to darken man's face before
God.

After Death

The four boards of the coffin lid
Heard all the dead man did.

The first curse was in his mouth,
Made of grave's mould and deadly drouth.

The next curse was in his head,
Made of God's work discomfited.

The next curse was in his hands,
Made out of two grave-bands.

The next curse was in his feet,
Made out of a grave-sheet.   10

'I had fair coins red and white,
And my name was as great light;

I had fair clothes green and red,
And strong gold bound round my head.

But no meat comes in my mouth,
Now I fare as the worm doth;

And no gold binds in my hair,
Now I fare as the blind fare.

My live thews were of great strength,
Now am I waxen a span's length;   20

My live sides were full of lust,
Now are they dried with dust.'

The first board spake and said:
'Is it best eating flesh or bread?'

The second answered it:
'Is wine or honey the more sweet?'

The third board spake and said:
'Is red gold worth a girl's gold head?'

The fourth made answer thus:
'All these things are as one with us.'   30

The dead man asked of them:
'Is the green land stained brown with flame?

Have they hewn my son for beasts to eat,
And my wife's body for beasts' meat?

Have they boiled my maid in a brass pan,
And built a gallows to hang my man?'

The boards said to him:
'This is a lewd thing that ye deem.

Your wife has gotten a golden bed,
All the sheets are sewn with red.   40

Your son has gotten a coat of silk,
The sleeves are soft as curded milk.

Your maid has gotten a kirtle new,
All the skirt has braids of blue.

Your man has gotten both ring and glove,
Wrought well for eyes to love.'

The dead man answered thus:
'What good gift shall God give us?'

The boards answered him anon:
'Flesh to feed hell's worm upon.'   50

From

Hymn to Proserpine

[AFTER THE PROCLAMATION IN ROME OF THE
CHRISTIAN FAITH]

Vicisti, Galilaee

I have lived long enough, having seen one thing, that love hath an
    end;
Goddess and maiden and queen, be near me now and befriend.
Thou art more than the day or the morrow, the seasons that laugh
    or that weep;
For these give joy and sorrow; but thou, Proserpina, sleep.
Sweet is the treading of wine, and sweet the feet of the dove;
But a goodlier gift is thine than foam of the grapes or love.
Yea, is not even Apollo, with hair and harpstring of gold,
A bitter God to follow, a beautiful God to behold?
I am sick of singing: the bays burn deep and chafe: I am fain
To rest a little from praise and grievous pleasure and pain.   10
For the Gods we know not of, who give us our daily breath,
We know they are cruel as love or life, and lovely as death.
O Gods dethroned and deceased, cast forth, wiped out in a day!
From your wrath is the world released, redeemed from your chains,
    men say.
New Gods are crowned in the city; their flowers have broken your
    rods;
They are merciful, clothed with pity, the young compassionate
    Gods.
But for me their new device is barren, the days are bare;
Things long past over suffice, and men forgotten that were.

Time and the Gods are at strife; ye dwell in the midst thereof,
Draining a little life from the barren breasts of love.   20
I say to you, cease, take rest; yea, I say to you all, be at peace,
Till the bitter milk of her breast and the barren bosom shall cease.
Wilt thou yet take all, Galilean? but these thou shalt not take,
The laurel, the palms and the paean, the breasts of the nymphs in
    the brake;
Breasts more soft than a dove's, that tremble with tenderer breath;
And all the wings of the Loves, and all the joy before death;
All the feet of the hours that sound as a single lyre,
Dropped and deep in the flowers, with strings that flicker like fire.
More than these wilt thou give, things fairer than all these things?
Nay, for a little we live, and life hath mutable wings.   30
A little while and we die; shall life not thrive as it may?
For no man under the sky lives twice, outliving his day.
And grief is a grievous thing, and a man hath enough of his tears:
Why should he labour, and bring fresh grief to blacken his years?
Thou hast conquered, O pale Galilean; the world has grown grey
    from thy breath;
We have drunken of things Lethean, and fed on the fullness of
    death.
Laurel is green for a season, and love is sweet for a day;
But love grows bitter with treason, and laurel outlives not May.
Sleep, shall we sleep after all? for the world is not sweet in the end;
For the old faiths loosen and fall, the new years ruin and rend.   40
Fate is a sea without shore, and the soul is a rock that abides;
But her ears are vexed with the roar and her face with the foam of
    the tides.
O lips that the live blood faints in, the leavings of racks and rods!
O ghastly glories of saints, dead limbs of gibbeted Gods!
Though all men abase them before you in spirit, and all knees bend,
I kneel not neither adore you, but standing, look to the end.

The Epitaph in Form of a Ballad

Men, brother men, that after us yet live,
   Let not your hearts too hard against us be;
For if some pity of us poor men ye give,
   The sooner God shall take of you pity.
   Here are we five or six strung up, you see,
And here the flesh that all too well we fed
Bit by bit eaten and rotten, rent and shred,
   And we the bones grow dust and ash withal;
Let no man laugh at us discomforted,
   But pray to God that he forgive us all.   10

If we call on you, brothers, to forgive,
   Ye should not hold our prayer in scorn, though we
Were slain by law; ye know that all alive
   Have not wit alway to walk righteously;
   Make therefore intercession heartily
With him that of a virgin's womb was bred,
That his grace be not as a dry well-head
   For us, nor let hell's thunder on us fall;
We are dead, let no man harry or vex us dead,
   But pray to God that he forgive us all.   20

The rain has washed and laundered us all five,
   And the sun dried and blackened; yea, perdie,
Ravens and pies with beaks that rend and rive
   Have dug our eyes out, and plucked off for fee
   Our beards and eyebrows; never are we free,

142

Not once, to rest; but here and there still sped,
Drive at its wild will by the wind's change led,
 More pecked of birds than fruits on garden-wall;
Men, for God's love, let no gibe here be said,
 But pray to God that he forgive us all.   30

Prince Jesus, that of all art lord and head,
Keep us, that hell be not our bitter bed;
 We have nought to do in such a master's hall.
Be not ye therefore of our fellowhead,
 But pray to God that he forgive us all.

COMMENTARY AND NOTES

WILLIAM BARNES

William Barnes was born in 1801 near Sturminster Newton, the market-town of the Vale of Blackmore in Dorset. He was the son of a small farmer, descended from a family that had once been landed gentry. In Barnes boyhood the Vale of Blackmore was a remote pastoral backwater where, as yet barely affected by the industrial revolution, the self-sufficient traditional rural life of England still continued practically unchanged from the seventeenth century.

He was educated at a village school. At the age of thirteen he was found a job (it was thought he was too delicate for farm-work) first in Sturminster then in Dorchester, the county capital, as a solicitor's clerk and copyist. But he found time to keep up his studies in Latin and Greek, and even to bring out his first two books of verse before he was twenty-one. These were in standard English, conventional in style, and printed locally at Dorchester. In 1823, when he was twenty-two, he took over a small school at Mere in Wiltshire not far from the borders of Dorset. Four years later he married Julia Miles, the daughter of an excise-officer at Dorchester. Her death twenty-five years later came as a crushing blow and led to some of Barnes' most moving poems, e.g. the well-known *Wife A-Lost* and *The Wold Wall*, besides others (for instance *The Bwoat*) based on memories of his courtship and married life.

As schoolmaster at Mere Barnes was able to satisfy his taste for learning. The range of his interests was extraordinary. He studied mathematics and helped General Shrapnel in his calculations for the shell named after him. Nor was he idle with his hands; he played the flute, violin, piano, and even practised engraving. But his passion was for languages. He made himself proficient in no less than seventeen, including Persian, Sanskrit, Hindustani, Arabic, Russian; kept a diary in Italian and another in Welsh. He became a home-made philologist, and published a number of books on the subject.

His *Philological Grammar* (1854) is an attempt to analyse the general laws which govern all languages. *Tiw, or A View of the Roots and Stems of English as a Teutonic Tongue* (1862) tries to reduce the English language 'to about fifty primary roots'. Late in life he published *English Speechcraft* (1878), the result of his lifelong preoccupation with the purifying, or Saxonising, of modern English; it contains some instructive as well as ludicrous coinings to replace words derived from Greek or Latin—e.g. 'fore-say' for 'preface', 'folkdom' for 'democracy', 'wordhead' for 'initial', 'hairbane' for 'depilatory', 'wort-lore' for 'botany', and 'push-wainling' for 'perambulator'. The list of Barnes' published works, apart from poetry, is long and formidable, ranging over books and essays on economics, mathematics, archaeology, sociology, and logic. Though he never crossed the sea and scarcely ever the borders of his native county (except for his stay at Mere and visits to Wales and Cambridge) he was in some respects the least parochial of Victorian poets.

In 1835 Barnes left Mere to open a second school in Dorchester. His first volume of Dorset dialect poems was published in London in 1844. Two years later he published *Poems Partly of Rural Life (In National English)*. *Hwomely Rhymes* followed in 1859, and in 1862 there was a third collection, *Poems of Rural Life in the Dorset Dialect*. 1868 saw the publication in both England and America of *Poems of Rural Life, in Common English*, some of which were 'translations' from poems originally written in dialect. Except for a selection of his unpublished poems which appeared in 1870, and the 1879 volume containing his three collections of dialect poems, this was the last book of verse he published in his lifetime.

In 1838 Barnes put his name on the books of St John's College, Cambridge, as a ten-years' man. He was ordained at Salisbury in 1847 and given the care of the tiny church of Whitcombe, though he did not get his B.D. degree until 1850. In 1852 his wife died and his school at Dorchester began to decline. For a while he found it difficult to make ends meet and support his family, but through the efforts of Tennyson, Arnold, Browning, Patmore and others he was relieved by the award of a Civil List pension of £70. At last, in 1862, he was given the living of Winterborne Came, three miles from Dorchester. There he remained vicar for nearly a quarter of a century till his death in 1886.

Barnes' life was peaceful but not secluded. He entered into the life he wrote about. As a schoolmaster he was an original and ingenious teacher stimulating in his pupils the wide-ranging curiosity he himself possessed to such a degree. Just as he evolved his own system of philology he evolved his own style of clerical dress, and would be seen going about his parish dressed in a cassock, wide-brimmed hat (which he sometimes exchanged for a Basque beret or a Turkish fez) black knee-breeches, black silk stockings and gold buckled shoes. Over this he would wear a South American poncho or a Scotch plaid; yet such was the natural dignity of the tall, white-bearded old clergyman with the impressive domed head that somehow he never managed to look ridiculous—even when walking down Dorchester High Street with a poker, shovel, and tongs slung over his back to save a tradesman the trouble of sending them. Barnes was gentle, innocent, unselfconscious, and intensely independent—qualities reflected again and again in his verse.

POETRY

The most remarkable thing about William Barnes' poems is their underivativeness. He once pointed out that he never read contemporary poets; he did not want to be trammelled with their thoughts and styles. Instead he modelled himself 'as regards only metre and rhyme' on poets of foreign literatures, just as Pound and Eliot were to prescribe in the next century when they laid the foundations of 'modern poetry'. Barnes shaped highly artificial verse-forms and metrical devices to meet the rhythm of ordinary spoken English or dialect speech. Among them were the Persian *ghazel*, Welsh *cynghannedd,* Italian *terza rima*, Hebrew parallelism, Anglo-Saxon alliteration. Such care and felicity went into his craftsmanship that no distortion or straining of language disturbs the effect of natural utterance characteristic of his best poems. In his verse he captured the intonation of ordinary speech as very few of his contemporaries succeeded in doing. This may best be seen in his dialect eclogues—*The Waggon A-Stooded*, or the one included here, *John, Jealous at Shroton Feäir*.

Barnes' poems are not distinguished by profundity of thought or social comment. They do not exhibit romantic passion but everyday feeling; and they succeed because they are never out of touch with reality. The images are first-hand and directly observed, the product of an acute and poetic eye—as in *Troubles of the Day*, where a toy boat sailed upon a windy pond is seen fluttering and 'tippling like a bird That tries to fly unfledged, to fly too soon'. The originality of Barnes' poems is often unnoticed because it is quiet and unselfconscious and never calls attention to itself—unlike, for instance, the poetry of Swinburne or Dylan Thomas.

Hopkins once complained that Barnes 'lacks fire'. The charge seems true if his poems are compared with those of his contemporary John Clare, the Northamptonshire peasant poet. But the combustion is there, none the less intense and thorough for being slow and hidden, like the heat in a charcoal-burner's stack. The industrial revolution, and the consequential agricultural revolution of the time of Barnes and Clare, led to the enclosure of common lands in a series of acts of parliament passed between the latter half of the eighteenth and the first four decades of the nineteenth century—acts which made it impossible for smallholding labourers to preserve their independence by keeping a pig or a cow or a goose or two. The enclosures meant the death of rural England. This is the underlying theme of the poetry of both Barnes

147

and Clare. In Barnes it is less explicit, though such eclogues as *The Common A-Took In, The 'Lotments, Rusticus Emigrans or Over the Sea to Settle,* and others, deal directly with the plight of the rural working-man. But Barnes' life was as tranquil as Clare's was tragic, and this is reflected in their verse; the agonized note in Clare's voice is not to be heard in the poems of Barnes, which have however a serene melancholy of their own. Clare's desolate protests are a cry of anguish; Barnes' humble memorials of traditional rural life—such poems as *Lydlinch Bells, The Old Farmhouse,* and many another— remain its elegy.

NOTES ON THE POEMS OF WILLIAM BARNES

15. BENIGHTED

Barnes' English poems, with which this selection begins, were written later than the dialect verses, but it seemed convenient to place them first as an introduction.

l.35. moonshade: i.e. shadow cast by the moonlight.

17. TROUBLES OF THE DAY

In this poem Barnes is imitating the parallelism of Hebrew poetry, in which images are balanced against one another: e.g.

> From the blood of the slain,
> From the fat of the mighty,
> The bow of Jonathan turned not back,
> The shield of Saul returned not empty.

See the repetitions in lines 2, 4, 11, 13, 22, 29.

18. BE'MI'STER

The Dorset dialect in which this and the following poems are written is not as difficult as it looks. Its constructions are nearer Anglo-Saxon than modern English (Barnes claimed it was a purer form of English). The main differences are the use of 'd' for 'th' ('drough' instead of 'through') 'v' for 'f' ('veet' instead of 'feet') 'z' for 's' ('zummer' instead of 'summer') and 'èn' in place of '—ing' (reachèn' for 'reaching') and certain differences of pronunciation that Barnes indicated by his spelling and accentuation.

l.1. Be'mi'ster: Beaminster, a small town in Dorset.

20. THE WOLD WALL

The refrain, 'Ah! well-a-day! O wall adieu!' is an imitation of the Welsh *cynghanedd*, in which consonantal sounds (in this case, WLD/WLD) are repeated in two parts of a line divided by a caesura. See also *Shaftesbury Feäir*.

21. WHEN BIRDS BE STILL

In Celtic poetry 'there is a kind of under-rhyme called *union*, which is the under-rhyming or rhyming of the last word or breath-sound in one line, with one in the middle of the following one' (Barnes). Here he employs it in the third and fourth, and again in the last two lines of each stanza, e.g.

> The sh'ill vaïced dog do stan' an' *bark*
> 'Ithin the *dark*, bezide the road

Note the skilful use of onomatopoeia in this stanza.

25. SHAFTESBURY FEÄIR

Another example of the use of *cynghanedd* is to be found in the seventh line of each stanza. Of this poem Hopkins wrote to Coventry Patmore: 'His employment of Welsh *cynghanedd* or chime I do not look on as quite successful. To tell the truth, I think I could do that better . . . I mean like *Paladore* and *Polly dear*, which is in my judgement more of a miss than a hit.'

*l.*1. *Paladore:* a traditional name for Shaftesbury, the British *Caer Paladr*.

27. ECLOGUE: JOHN, JEALOUS AT SHROTON FEÄIR

This eclogue recreates with humour and economy the atmosphere of a country fair. There is a timelessness about the situation: the girl in a pet because her best clothes have been ruffled by the crowd, the clumsy efforts of her two escorts to put things right and restore her good humour with a compliment; the flirtation with a rustic gallant; her lover's jealousy and sulks, and her brother's anxious attempt to pour oil on troubled waters. Barnes exhibits an observation as exact as Chaucer's; his small touches, deftly placed, provide the same vivid and authentic effect.

*ll.*3–4. 'Fancy plunging in when people are squeezing as tight as a cheese-press on a vat of cheese!'

*l.*7. 'My bonnet's like a bundle, beaten up into a shapeless lump.'

ARTHUR HUGH CLOUGH

Arthur Hugh Clough was born at Liverpool on New Year's Day, 1819, the son of a cotton-merchant of good family who soon afterwards emigrated to South Carolina with his wife and children. But at the age of ten Clough was brought back to England to be educated at Rugby School. There Dr Thomas Arnold, Matthew Arnold's father, had just begun his famous headmastership which was to 'change the face of education all through the public schools of England'. Very soon Clough became Dr Arnold's prize pupil. As his parents lived in America, Clough had little home-life while a boy; it may be said he had no real boyhood at all, for many of his holidays were spent with the Arnold family, which perhaps gave him too little respite from the atmosphere of high ideals and moral tension that characterized Dr Arnold's Rugby.

In 1837 he went up to Oxford, the storm centre of the Tractarian controversy (also known as the Oxford Movement) then at its zenith. The Anglican church was split between the Church Liberals (championed by Dr Arnold) who believed in religion based on rationalism, and the Tractarians, the party of intellectual reformers led by John Henry Newman, who believed in the divine authority of the Church. W. G. Ward, one of Newman's leading disciples (and who later became one of the first Tractarians to go over to Rome) was Clough's tutor at Balliol. Ward formed a close, somewhat over-powering friendship with Clough. Exerting much the same degree of moral pressure on Clough as the headmaster of Rugby, though in a rather different direction, the effect of Ward's speculative turn of mind was thoroughly unsettling. 'There goes Ward,' it used to be said, 'mystifying poor Clough and persuading him that he must either believe *nothing* or accept the whole of Church doctrine.' No wonder Clough ended up as a sceptic.

Clough, the prize scholar, disappointed all expectations by failing to take a first when he sat for his degree. As a result he was not offered a Balliol Fellowship, but obtained one at Oriel in 1842. Among his colleagues was Matthew Arnold, who was elected a Fellow three years later. In 1848, assailed by scruples over subscribing to the 39 Articles (as all University Fellows were then required to do) Clough resigned his Fellowship.

During the next three years he wrote his three principal poems: *The Bothie of Tober-na-Vuolich, Amours de Voyage,* and the fragmentary *Dipsychus.* He travelled to Paris, which had just experienced the revolution of 1848, and the following year spent several months in Rome, where he witnessed its siege by the French and the flight of Garibaldi. These events provided him with material for *Amours de Voyage*, which he began in the same year.

Clough was not rich and had his mother and sisters to support. His scruples over the 39 Articles made it difficult for him to obtain the kind of academic post for which he was qualified. However he obtained the headship of University Hall, a non-sectarian hostel for students, and later the Chair of English at University College, London. But he had no great enthusiasm for 'Doubting Hall' as Matthew Arnold nicknamed it, and tried unsuccessfully for an academic post in Australia. In 1852, encouraged by his friend Emerson, the American philosopher-poet, he visited Boston. There he began a translation of Plutarch and toyed with the idea of starting a school. After much vacillation he returned to England and accepted an examinership in the Education Office. In 1854 he married Blanche Smith, a cousin of Florence Nightingale.

After his marriage Clough wrote little poetry, and what he did write was markedly inferior to his earlier work. He became more and more involved with his job in the Civil Service. On Florence Nightingale's return from the Crimea he became her helper and amanuensis, reading the proofs of her monumental memorandum on hospital reform in his spare time from the office. In fact this formidable woman made Clough her dogsbody, till in 1860 his health cracked under the strain. He took a long leave, but in 1861 died of a stroke in Florence at the early age of forty-two.

POETRY

Of all the Victorian poets Clough stands out as one who in mood and temper seems closer to the twentieth than the nineteenth century. The detached, ironic, astringent, and debunking turn of mind expressed in Clough's best poetry has the modern ring; there are passages in *Amours de Voyage* which in tone and diction, and particularly in the way the tempo of ordinary speech is captured and reproduced, remind one of Laforgue, Ezra Pound, and T. S. Eliot. Michael Roberts, in the preface to *The Faber Book of Modern Verse*, appears to claim Clough as much as G. M. Hopkins as one of the forerunners of modern poetry.

It would seem that the self-doubt and introspectiveness which are Clough's chief attributes stopped him from becoming a poet of the first rank, as he might have been had he recognized or at any rate believed in his vocation as a poet. Sceptical of, even jeering at, the middle-class values of the nineteenth century, Clough nevertheless subscribed—or rather submitted—to them in practice. *Dipsychus* is a reflection of this conflict. It is significant that his three important poems were written in the vagabond years between his resigning the Oriel Fellowship and accepting another academic post in London. His last long work, *Mari Magno* (a collection of tales in verse, written after his marriage) is distinguished not only by appallingly crude versification but by an endorsement of morbid Victorian morality difficult to reconcile with the subtle and ironic probing of accepted opinions that one finds in his earlier poetry.

Clough and Matthew Arnold are complementary and opposed. Whereas Clough's friend Arnold was a gay dandiacal young man who surprised everyone with the gravity of his poems, it was the other way round with Clough. He was a serious youth whom his headmaster had nearly succeeded in turning into a prig; who had been subjected to further moral buffeting from his tutor at Oxford; who had been involved in the theological controversy of the time; and who had resigned an Oriel Fellowship on a point of conscience. Suddenly this solemn young man published a long poem with an odd title—*The Bothie of Tober-na-Vuolich*. It was the last kind of thing to be expected from an earnest, over-conscientious youth like Clough: a dandiacal poem about a reading-party in the Highlands and an undergraduate's love-affair with a shepherd's daughter. Even the metre was dandiacal, for Clough chose none of the accepted verse-forms of the day but wrote it in impudently colloquial hexameters. Much shrewd social comment disguised itself behind a light and almost flippant tone, as well as a surprisingly profound psychological understanding of the nature of women. Neither the sentimentality nor vulgarity of feeling that wreck other nineteenth-century 'novels in verse' which attempt a contemporary setting, is present in *The Bothie*, or in Clough's next long poem, *Amours de Voyage*. As in Coventry Patmore's *The Angel in the House*, the gothic element—i.e. over-melodramatic plot and incident—that makes, for instance, Mrs Browning's otherwise very readable *Aurora Leigh* both unreal and absurd, is totally absent. What is admirable is the lightness of touch and the poet's ironic angle of glance.

Seen against the background of the general run of Victorian poetry, *Amours de Voyage* is remarkable for its modernity. In its understatements and subtleties it belongs to the era of Henry James rather than that of Dickens. The scene of the poem is Rome during its siege by the French in 1849. The story (told in the form of letters from the various characters) seems as tenuous as the plot of a *nouvelle vague* film. Claude, an English tourist, a somewhat bored and undecided youth (there are similarities between him and the middle-aged protagonist of T. S. Eliot's *The Love Song of J. Alfred Prufrock*) meets an English family (middle-class but slightly lower than he in the social scale), is of service to them during the siege, decides he is in love with one of the daughters, does nothing, then makes up his mind to propose. Meanwhile the family have gone on to Florence; he follows; finds them gone; and so on till he finally abandons the search and reflects it was probably all for the best. On this slight web Clough hangs delicately mocking yet penetrating analyses of such questions as the nature of will and action; saturnine, startlingly *blasé* disquisitions on war, patriotism, class-nuances, social duty and so on. It is not a great poem—Clough never wrote a 'great' poem—but where more self-consciously portentous Victorian masterpieces have faded in our eyes, *Amours de Voyage* retains life, immediacy, and freshness.

Clough's next poem was left unfinished. In intention *Dipsychus* is far more ambitious than either of his two preceding poems, but unlike them it is not properly unified, and as a whole it fails to come off. Its versification is stumbling and uneven. The poem is set in Venice, and is a duologue between a young student and a Spirit, who may or may not be Mephistopheles: as Clough says in his epilogue, 'perhaps he wasn't a devil after all. That's the beauty of the poem; nobody can say . . . The thing which it is attempted to represent is the conflict between the tender conscience and the world. Now, the over-tender conscience will, of course, exaggerate the wickedness of the world . . .' Clough was not attempting a conventional exercise on the Faust theme, for the two protagonists are a dichotomy and really represent two contradictory sides of Clough. It is in a way a psychological analysis of himself. Spirit and student wander through Venice, the one tempting, the other resisting temptation—but having his arguments astringently debunked all the same; for the Spirit gets rather the better of it. The Spirit goads the student to action—any action; but as Clough wrote in *Amours de Voyage*, 'action/Is a most dangerous thing'.

What is generally to be found in Clough's best poems is usually absent from Victorian poetry—a gaiety of intellect: an adult intellectual seriousness that does not take itself too seriously. He could not, for example, have written the unconsciously comic lines of one of Arnold's Marguerite poems (Arnold is about to visit the lady):

> Again I spring to make my choice;
> Again in tones of ire,
> I hear a God's tremendous voice,
> 'Be counsell'd, and retire.'

Though Clough often took himself portentously in the Victorian manner. His well-known poem, *Easter Day*, with its refrain, 'Christ is not risen!' expresses his loss of religious faith in a tone not far from hysteria. Yet of Victorian poets it is Clough who is the real heir of Byron—the Byron of *Don Juan*. Though he lacks Byron's energy and force Clough has a good deal of his urbane irony and airy manner. His psychological insight is more profound. In *The Bothie of Tober-na-Vuolich* Elsie's speech to Philip, with its remarkable image of the bridge, bears witness to a penetrating discernment of the psychological response of a woman to passionate love that was quite beyond Byron's capacity, and indeed of most nineteenth-century poets or novelists.

Notes on the Poems of Arthur Hugh Clough

31. THE SHADOW

Though a fragment and unfinished, this poem is one of the best and most ironic expressions of Clough's agnosticism and his sardonic view of the hypocrisy with which the Christian religion was regarded and turned into use by the worldly, and by the clergy of the Roman Catholic and Anglican Churches.

l.5. the Greek poet: Homer. A reference to Book XI of the *Odyssey*, where Ulysses calls up the spirits of his dead companions.

ll.86-7 Butler and Paley: Joseph Butler (1692-1752). Bishop of Durham, wrote the *Analogy of Religion*; William Paley (1743-1805) an English divine, wrote *Views of the Evidences of Christianity*, both famous works which seek to prove the truth of the Christian religion.

34. THE LATEST DECALOGUE

An ironic commentary on the Ten Commandments.

35. *From* THE BOTHIE OF TOBER-NA-VUOLICH

Philip, a young Oxford undergraduate with Socialistic views, is one of a reading-party in Scotland; he has just declared his love to Elspie, the daughter of a Highland shepherd. This passage is remarkable for the insight it shows into the psychology of women; it is equally remarkable for the way in which it combines poetry of a high order while preserving a natural conversational tone in keeping with the realism of the rest of the poem.

36. *From* AMOURS DE VOYAGE

This poem was written almost contemporaneously with the siege of Rome by the French, which forms its background. The story is told in a series of letters, mostly written by Claude, a young English tourist; Claude is in many ways Clough's self-portrait. The extracts are all taken from Claude's letters to a friend in England.

l.19 assujettisement: constraint.

l.33 Bernini: Giovanni Lorenzo Bernini (1598-1680) one of the greatest baroque sculptors, was responsible for the colonnade of St Peter's, and also for many of the tombs inside.

Often printed by itself, this poem is extracted from *Dipsychus*, where it is supposed to be spoken by the ironical Spirit (who may or may not be Mephistopheles) to the Student.

41. SPECTATOR AB EXTRA

Also from *Dipsychus*, where it is another of the Spirit's disquisitions. The poem was printed as it stands in the posthumous 1862 edition of Clough's poems, where *Dipsychus* is omitted; but the version in *Dipsychus* is considerably shorter.

MATTHEW ARNOLD

LIFE

Matthew Arnold was born at the Thames-side village of Laleham, near Staines, on 24th December 1822. He was the eldest son of Dr Thomas Arnold, who was soon to become headmaster of Rugby, where his educational reforms—with their insistence on character-building and high ideals—were to leave an indelible mark on the temper of the coming Victorian era. In 1833 Dr Arnold moved to Fox How in the Lake District, a house not far from Rydal Mount where his friend Wordsworth was living. After a short period at Winchester, Matthew was sent to school under his father at Rugby. Unlike Clough he was not exactly a model pupil; but he did well enough, winning the school poetry prize with some Byronic verses, and a scholarship to Balliol, which he entered in 1841. The following year his father died suddenly of angina pectoris.

At Oxford Arnold was a lighthearted undergraduate who spent more time than he should have in fishing, boating, riding to harriers, or wandering among the Cumnor hills with his friend Clough. Like Clough, but from different causes, he failed to obtain a first in Classics. However he won the Newdigate Prize for a poem on Cromwell. In 1845 he was elected to an Oriel Fellowship.

Next year he travelled on the Continent, paying a visit to George Sand on his way to Switzerland; returning, he spent a month in Paris, fascinated by Rachel's acting. Soon after he came back to Oxford Clough was writing to a friend, 'Matt is full of Parisianism; theatres in general, and Rachel in special; he enters the room with a chanson of Béranger's on his lips . . . his carriage shows him in fancy parading the Rue de Rivoli; and his hair is guiltless of English scissors'. Arnold—it may have been a reaction against his father's moral earnestness—was a dandy; elegant, urbane, almost a fop, yet rescued from foppery and superciliousness by an attractive blend of good nature, wit, high spirits, and charm. He did not long remain at Oxford. In April 1847 he became private secretary to Lord Lansdowne, an influential Liberal statesman in Lord John Russell's ministries. For the next two years Arnold visited Switzerland each September, probably in pursuit of his unsuccessful love affair with an unknown woman—the 'daughter of France' to whom the 'Marguerite' poems in his volume of 1852 are addressed. But in 1850 he fell in love with Frances Wightman, the daughter of a Judge of the Queen's Bench. Judge Wightman at first opposed the marriage, but finally consented to it provided Arnold obtained a secure and adequate income. In 1851 Lord Lansdowne made Arnold's marriage possible by appointing him to an Inspectorship of Schools in the Department of Education. He held this post, which involved much hard work and much travelling up and down the country visiting scho ls, for more than thirty-five years.

Arnold's first collection of poems, *The Strayed Reveller and Other Poems*, was published anonymously in 1849. It made no impression and was withdrawn after the sale of a very few copies. In 1852 he published *Empedocles on Etna, and Other Poems*, which did little better (*The Times* reviewer superbly commenting 'He is disgusted with the world; a state of mind with which we have no sympathy whatever'). The following year he published a new edition of his poems, excluding *Empedocles*, and including a preface which explained the reason for this omission and went on to outline Arnold's theory of poetry. This preface was Arnold's first essay in criticism. In 1855 he published *Poems, Second Series*—substantially the same book with the addition of some new work. This was followed in 1852 by *Merope*, a classical tragedy in verse. Nine years later he published what was to be his last collection of new poetry. It was called *New Poems*, though many had been written years earlier. After its publication Arnold was to write no more poetry to speak of, beyond a funeral ode for Dean Stanley and some embarassing verses on the deaths of various pet animals.

In 1857 Arnold was elected to the Chair of Poetry at Oxford, which he held for the next ten years. His predecessors had been undistinguished; Arnold was the first Professor of Poetry to be permitted to give his lectures in English instead of Latin. This was the beginning of Arnold's serious involvement with literary criticism and his offensive against the provincialism of English critical standards and the philistinism of the English middle-classes. He published his first three lectures, *On Translating Homer,* in 1861, followed by *Essays in Criticism* (1865), and *On The Study of Celtic Literature* (1868). Not all his writing was concerned with literary criticism. In the sixties he published several works on education, and later turned his attention to social and political problems (*Culture and Anarchy*, 1869, *Friendship's Garland*, 1871) and finally to the question of religious belief (*Literature and Dogma*, 1870, *God and the Bible*, 1875, *Last Essays on Church and Religion*, 1877). As he grew older Arnold saw himself, in his educational, social, and religious criticism, as a reformer like his father and the continuator of his work.

In 1883 Arnold went to America to give a lecture tour, partly to pay his son's Oxford debts. Three years later he paid a second visit to see his married daughter. In 1886 he resigned his Inspectorship of Schools. His retirement did not last long; in 1888, on his way to meet his daughter at Liverpool, he leapt over a low fence while running to catch a tram and dropped dead of heart failure.

POETRY

In some ways Arnold is the dominant poet of those represented in this anthology. He is the only one who formulated an aesthetic; and he wrote some of the finest—or at any rate the most exquisitely fashioned—poems of his time. He had an ear second only to Tennyson's and an intellect superior to Browning's. Yet he is not quite their equal as a poet. This may be due to the fact that he never fully projected himself into his poetry—there is a whole side of Arnold's personality that is totally absent from his verse. Arnold the melancholy, Arnold the wistful, Arnold the pessimist, Arnold the doubter, Arnold the lover and even Arnold the critic and pedagogue are all there: but what of the other side of Arnold—which we find in of all places his prose criticism and polemics—Arnold the dandy, teasing Arnold, Arnold the debonair, Arnold the charmer, the elegant goodnatured wit? It may be he took poetry too portentously, unlike his friend Clough (it is significant that neither of the two really appreciated the other's verse). Arnold saw himself as a prophet of the modern age; yet it can be said that excepting D. G. Rossetti and Swinburne, of all the poets in this book Arnold's poetry is the most essentially of its time. In the style and tenor of his verse he sought the virtues of Classicism (Homer was his touchstone): yet his best poems show that the mind and heart behind them belong to a Romantic.

The reasoning faculty that served Arnold so well in his criticism tended in the end to blunt or atrophy, or at least to cause him to distrust, the intuitive faculty which is even more necessary for the making of a poem. It is thus probably true that his criticism, valuable as it may have been in confronting complacent mediocrity with the highest standards, and shaking up the provincial smugness of the Victorians, strangled Arnold's own poetry. The stream completely dried up by the time he was forty-five. And this he may intuitively have foreshadowed, as John Heath-Stubbs has hinted, in Callicles' song from *Empedocles on Etna* about the faun Marsyas vanquished by Apollo— 'the Dionysian singer silenced by the Apollonian intellect'. Arnold worried about 'high seriousness', the 'eternal objects of poetry' which are 'actions; human actions'; making it an essential prerequisite for a poet to 'select an excellent action' for his poem. But he forgot it is not enough to choose an excellent action if it is not one that does not involve the poet's own deepest feelings, the conflicts that exist on the level of the subconscious—and to do this the poet needs his faculty of intuition. Hence Arnold's two major set-pieces in 'the grand style'—*Sohrab and Rustum*, and *Balder Dead*, with their elaborate Homeric similes—remain little more than academic *tours-de-force* despite passages of fine writing that are often of extreme felicity. Even the famous closing passage of *Sohrab and Rustum,* the long Homeric simile of the Oxus debouching into the Aral sea, is paradoxically as un-Homeric as may be; for it projects, in the Romantic manner, a symbolism, an emotional identification with landscape, of which no 'classical' poet could have been capable.

It is not in such deliberately conceived poems, exercises in 'the grand style' which Arnold defined and advocated in his prose criticism, that his most vital poetry resides. Nor does one find it in his imitations of classical Greek plays such as *Merope* or *Empedocles on Etna*, where Empedocles, the disconsolate philosopher, expounds his dispirited, ratiocinative vision of a neutral universe without gods (or with gods indifferent to man's fate) wherein

> Man errs not that he dreams
> His welfare his true aim,
> He errs because he dreams
> The world does but exist that welfare to bestow.

Rather it is to be found in those almost *malgre lui* Romantic poems, for example in the songs of Callicles in the above play. Callicles counterpoints the prosy jeremaids of the philosopher with lyrics that express an affirmation of delight—an intuitive, essentially Romantic apprehension of the nature of reality, with all its irrational cruelties and splendours, to which Arnold's conscious intellect was not to be reconciled. That vision was even more powerfully expressed in *The Strayed Reveller,* one of the earliest and strangest of Arnold's poems. In this poem a tranced and drunken youth, one of Circe's victims, describes the world as seen by the Gods, and by the poets who, unlike the Gods, must also endure what they see—

> Such a price
> The Gods exact for song;
> To become what we sing.

But Arnold was rarely to strike the Dionysian note. His Romanticism is a sort of plangent resignation—at worst, 'a pleasing melancholy' (his own comment). It may be seen at its best in *The Scholar Gipsy* and its companion,

Thyrsis, with their half-symbolic half-visionary landscapes, like the paintings of Samuel Palmer; their backward look to a lost pastoral world, to the figure of the questing solitary turning his back on the modern age, to the dead poet (in elegizing Clough in *Thyrsis* Arnold was also elegizing himself) silenced by it.

NOTES ON THE POEMS OF MATTHEW ARNOLD

45. *From* THE STRAYED REVELLER

The Strayed Reveller was the title-poem of Arnold's first volume of verse. It is an extraordinary production; the rapid, irregular, rhymeless verses are quite unlike anything in Victorian poetry. The poem draws a parallel between the ecstatic intoxication of the votaries of Dionysius (here called by his ritual name, Iacchus) and the experience of poets in the act of creation.

The enchantress Circe finds a youth drunken with her magic wine asleep in her portico. The Youth is a symbol of Dionysiac inspiration and of the poet. Circe calls Ulysses to see him—Ulysses representing the experienced man of action, the type of active life. To Ulysses the Youth describes, in a sequence of brilliant images, the vision of the world seen by the Gods—the imaginative apprehension of reality that is granted to 'the wise bards also' and for which a price is exacted—'to become what we sing.'

l.6. Tiresias: The blind seer who lived to a great age and foretold the doom of Thebes.

l.54. Chorasmian stream: The river Oxus, which flows into the Aral Sea. Arnold's description of the Indian on his floating island and the ferry over the Oxus comes from Captain Sir Alexander Burnes' *Travels into Bokhara.*

l.91. Hera: The wife of Zeus.

l.99. Lapithae, and Theseus: Theseus, the founder of Thebes, helped the Lapiths in their battle with the drunken Centaurs—half-men, half-horse—at the wedding of the Lapith king.

l.102. Alcmena's dreadful son: Hercules.

l.132. Silenus: A satyr, tutor and companion of Dionysius.

51. ISOLATION

Isolation was the original title of this poem, which became fifth in a group of lyrics Arnold entitled *Switzerland.* They are known as the 'Marguerite' poems, from the name of the unknown woman to whom they are addressed. Arnold may have met her on his first trip to Switzerland when he was twenty-five. From the poems it seems clear that she was French; that there was some obstacle (Arnold says, 'Our different pasts') that prevented him from pursuing the affair. She has been variously conjectured to have been a chambermaid, a governess, an aristocrat, or even an actress. All that is certain is that she existed. Many other poems of Arnold's seem to have been inspired by this affair—e.g. *The Forsaken Merman.*

52. DOVER BEACH

The theme of this poem is the ebbing of religious faith and Arnold's consequent perplexity and despair. All that is left to hold on to is human love. The reference to Sophocles is probably to his *Antigone* (lines 583 *et seq.*)

53. *From* STANZAS FROM THE GRANDE CHARTREUSE

The lines printed here form the central part of this poem. Arnold visited the monastery of the Grande Chartreuse while on his honeymoon in 1851. The poem begins with the approach to the monastery, and goes on to describe the monks at their conventual mass, and the buildings, chapel, library, and garden of the Grande Chartreuse. At this point the extract begins. Arnold sees the monastery (an anachronism in the modern world) as a symbol of the religious faith in which he no longer believes or finds intellectually acceptable; and yet

> Wandering between two worlds, one dead,
> The other powerless to be born

he has nothing to put in its place; while

> Achilles ponders in his tent,
> The kings of modern thought are dumb

i.e. the men of action and thinkers of his time offer no help either.

*l.*39. *sciolists:* half-scholars, who pretend to knowledge.

*l.*75. *Aetolian shore:* Byron died at Missolinghi, in the province of Aetolia in Greece.

56. THE SCHOLAR-GIPSY

The Scholar-Gipsy and *Thyrsis* are closely linked, though the former appeared in 1853 and the latter in 1867. Arnold evolved—probably after studying Keats' Odes—an intricate, highly effective rhyming pattern for his stanzas, which is repeated in *Thyrsis.* In each case the pastoral setting is the same—the country round the Cumnor Hills, where Clough and Arnold used to wander in their University days. In *The Scholar-Gipsy* the season is high summer; in *Thyrsis,* appropriately, it is late autumn. The symbolism is vague, but it seems clear that the Scholar Gipsy is Arnold's *alter ego,* the pure and dedicated poet he would have wished to be were it not for the pressure of the age in which he lived.

*l.*1. *shepherd:* It is not clear who this shepherd is, or what he is doing in the poem; perhaps a reference to Clough?

*l.*31. *Glanvil's book: The Vanity of Dogmatizing,* by Joseph Glanvill (1636–1680). This work attempts to show how philosophical scepticism may be used as a support for religious faith. Not a surprising book for Arnold to be reading at the height of the Oxford Movement! The passage quoted from it and printed at the head of the poem was much condensed and edited by Arnold to suit his purposes.

*l.*182. *amongst us one:* According to Arnold, this was Goethe. It has been suggested that Tennyson may have been meant. Tennyson had recently been appointed Poet Laureate (hence the line 'takes . . . his seat upon the intellectual throne'; 'intellectual throne' being a phrase from Tennyson's *Palace of Art*) after the appearance of *In Memoriam,* his elegy for Arthur Hallam; lines 185–6 may be a reference to it. They are certainly an apt if sardonic description of *In Memoriam.*

*l.*208. *Dido:* a reference to the *Aeneid,* Book VI, where Aeneas (the 'false friend') meets the ghost of Dido in the underworld; she had killed herself when he abandoned her at Carthage.

*ll.*220–240. The long Homeric simile of the Tyrian trader is famous, but seems to have little to do with the poem, which really closes with the preceding stanza. Arnold often tried to end his poems on a more or less cheerful note. But the simile of a Tyrian trader driven from his markets by Greek competition to seek fresh ones seems hardly appropriate to the unworldly Scholar Gipsy.

64. THYRSIS

This is Arnold's last major poem. In this elegy for his friend Clough he seems to be making his own farewell to poetry.

*l.*85. *cross the unpermitted ferry's flow:* i.e. the Styx, the river bordering the Underworld where Pluto reigns with his queen Proserpine.

*l.*167. *Arno vale:* Florence, where Clough died and is buried, stands on the river Arno.

*l.*184. *Lityerses song:* A harvest song sung by corn-reapers in ancient times. Lityerses was a king of Phrygia who used to challenge strangers to a reaping-contest; if they lost the penalty was death. Daphnis was the Sicilian shepherd who invented bucolic poetry. In one legend he was rescued from Lityerses by Hercules; in another he is said to have been struck blind for his faithlessness by a jealous nymph. His father Hermes carried him up to heaven.

COVENTRY PATMORE

Coventry Patmore was born on 23rd July 1823 at Woodford in Essex. His father, Peter George Patmore, had inherited a small fortune, and was an atheist and a literary dilettante—a sort of Bohemian dandy who had been acquainted with Keats and his circle as well as the fashionable Lady Blessington. But his enthusiasm for poetry was real: and he was responsible for the reverence in which his son Coventry always held the vocation of poet. Patmore senior enthusiastically encouraged his son's ambition to become one. But in 1845 he lost his fortune through speculating in railway shares. Thus the young Coventry Patmore, after having been brought up to expect a life of gentlemanly affluence, was suddenly faced with the prospect of having to earn his living. One of his father's friends (Richard Monckton Milnes, the biographer of Keats, who afterwards became Lord Houghton) found him a post in the library of the British Museum, where he remained for nearly twenty years.

In 1847 Coventry Patmore married Emily Augusta Andrews, the daughter of a Congregational minister. The marriage was ideally happy, and she bore him six children. About this time Patmore met D. G. Rossetti and the Pre-Raphaelite Brotherhood. Though Patmore wrote articles for the Pre-Raphaelite magazine *The Germ,* and got Ruskin to write his famous letter to *The Times* defending the paintings of Millais and the Pre-Raphaelites (which eventually made their fortunes) he did not join the Brotherhood. During these years he wrote and published *The Angel in the House,* his 'domestic epic' in celebration of marriage. The four parts of this poem, including its sequel *The Victories of Love,* appeared separately between 1854 and 1862. It was immediately popular, sold widely, and established Patmore's reputation.

In 1862 his wife died. Patmore's world fell to pieces. Two years later he travelled to Rome and there became a convert to the Roman Catholic Church. This was no sudden emotional conversion but the logical outcome of his religious thoughts and beliefs. Indeed it had been foreboded by his wife, herself a passionate Protestant. She had also urged him to remarry: and this Patmore did a few months after his conversion. His second wife was Maria Caroline Byles, a modest, deeply religious woman, so retiring that when Patmore proposed to her while she was visiting Rome with a paid travelling-companion, he was under the impression that Miss Byles was the travelling-companion. In fact she possessed a considerable fortune. Discovering his mistake, Patmore wished to withdraw; but friends overcame his scruples and the marriage took place in 1864. Soon afterwards Patmore retired from his post at the British Museum. In 1866 he bought an estate in Sussex, where he settled down to the life of a patriarch and landowner. Here he wrote the series of odes round the memory of his dead wife which he published in 1877 under the title of *The Unknown Eros*. This volume did not repeat the success of *The Angel in the House*, perhaps because people did not understand its transcendental philosophy of love or the metrical innovations it introduced; or more simply, because of the sentimental disapproval 'the poet of marriage' incurred among the Victorian public by taking a second wife.

In 1880 Maria Patmore, who had been semi-invalid for most of her marriage, died. A year later Patmore married again (as Valery Larbaud remarked, the poet of marriage could not long remain a widower). His third wife was Harriet Robson, who had been his children's governess during the illness of Maria Patmore. She was to survive him and bear him one more child.

After his third marriage Patmore wrote no more poetry but turned to prose, publishing in 1889 *Principle in Art*, a collection of critical essays notable for their clarity and independence of judgement. This was followed by another collection of essays, *Religio Poetae*, and by *The Rod, the Root, and the Flower*, which is largely concerned with the analogy between human and divine love—the central thesis of all Patmore's work. The latter is a unique book and has often been regarded as Patmore's masterpiece. All Patmore's prose is spare and pithy; here his thought is at its most compressed, and set forth in short paragraph-length meditations, or in epigrammatic statements and aphorisms.

In Patmore's later years he was an almost forgotten poet. However he became friendly with Gerard Manley Hopkins, who was later to be recognized as the most original and perhaps the greatest of Victorian poets. Patmore deferred to the younger man's judgement to such an extent that he even burned the MS of one of his prose books because Hopkins had expressed a reservation about it. Another of Patmore's late friendships was with Alice Meynell; but it ended painfully for Patmore, who seems to have wished it to be more of an *amitié amoureuse* than the poetess bargained for, till in the end she declined his visits. Patmore survived his friend Hopkins by seven years, and died at Lymington in 1896.

POETRY

By a mathematical coincidence each of Patmore's marriages lasted almost exactly fifteen years; and his work, it has been noted, divides itself into three exactly corresponding periods. *The Angel in the House* and its sequel was written during the lifetime of the first Mrs Patmore; *The Unknown Eros* belongs to the reign of the second; while after his third marriage Patmore stopped writing poetry altogether and turned to prose.

The Angel in the House is written in light, rapid iambic octosyllabics; its language is clear, fluent, and simple; it is witty and it is readable. These qualities conceal—perhaps too effectively—a wide reading in philosophy and an intellectual toughness of thought. Its subject is marriage: and Patmore showed considerable audacity in chosing for the thesis of a long and serious poem what was, and is, regarded as a theme for music-hall jokes. The difficulties it offered were formidable, and on the whole Patmore managed them very well.

For one thing, the nineteenth-century idea of romantic love (to which he himself more or less subscribed) is at bottom antithetical to the institution of marriage. The romantic view of love has its roots in the artificial medieval convention of '*l'amour courtois*' (courtly love) celebrated by the Provençal troubadours. One of the strictest tenets of '*l'amour courtois*' was the incompatability of romantic love and marriage—this was principally because feudal nobles always married for political or financial reasons. This tenet can be seen to have survived with various modifications to ourown times, and still operates to the disadvantage of Patmore's poem. Again, marriage cannot be properly treated in a poem or anywhere else without bringing in the subject of sex, which in Patmore's day was wholly taboo. While Patmore was certainly one of the few Victorian poets who neither avoided nor sentimentalized sexuality, his treatment of it is somewhat rarefied. This may have been inevitable, for though Patmore was neither puritan nor prude his vision of sexual love was that of a mystic. He saw it in terms of an analogy of divine love. Though the marriage that *The Angel in the House* celebrates is a human marriage, it also allegorizes the relation between the human and the divine: the 'Angel' of the title is meant to be understood in a theological as well as a metaphorical sense. Together with its sequel, *The Victories of Love*, the poem sets out to depict the whole character of married love. Patmore balanced the mysticism of its central idea with a down-to-earth, even banal, realism. Thus its setting is contemporary—a rare thing in Victorian poetry, at least in combination with successful handling—while the two protagonists of the poem are a perfectly ordinary middle-class couple. (One cannot help feeling they are a shade too comfortable, but then the Victorian middle-class *was* comfortable). Moreover the story of their courtship and marriage is kept as commonplace and uneventful as possible. Patmore is not afraid of the commonplace, as so many Victorian poets were; in fact it may be said he is a master of the banal, which he deploys with humour and effect to show the interdependence of the mundane and spiritual in ordinary daily life. Yet Patmore's ironic, often deadpan humour has been mistaken for bathos by serious souls. In *The Angel in the House* marriage is idealized but not sentimentalized, though sentiment—as distinct from sentimentality—is given its due place. The poem contains many shrewd insights on the nature of women and the relation of the sexes: these show Patmore to be no mean psychologist.

Its sequel, *The Victories of Love*, is a study of an unhappy marriage: or rather of a badly suited couple achieving eventual happiness through marriage. The device is used of telling the story in the form of letters written by six of the characters. Though Patmore makes great efforts to catch the colloquial tone of ordinary correspondence and often succeeds, the impression of artificiality remains. Perhaps the use of rhymed couplets is the trouble here, for the same device of telling a story in a series of letters is used successfully by Clough in *Amours de Voyage*, whose conversational hexameters suggest the natural style of a familiar correspondence more convincingly.

The Unknown Eros, though completely different in form, technique, and even in diction from *The Angel in the House* and its sequel, is on a deeper level a continuation and development of their theme. Many of the odes that make up its first part are elegiac meditations on Patmore's dead wife; with these are mingled one or two savage political satires directed impartially against the Tory Disraeli and the Liberal Gladstone. Nevertheless *The Unknown Eros* is not, as would seem, a collection of miscellaneous poems. The various odes are placed in relation to one another, and together (as Osbert Burdett points out) they outline the whole pedigree of love in all its aspects. The first book opens with a series of odes in which Love is symbolized in nature, then in terms of human feeling, of social action (hence the 'political odes') and philosophy. The odes of the second book are more ecstatic and transcendental; they deal with the soul's union with God. Some of the finest English mystical poetry is to be found in these odes, which have been said to constitute a minor *Paradiso*.

In technique the odes represent a new departure in English poetry, though based on the madrigals of William Drummond of Hawthornden and the 'pindaric' odes of Abraham Cowley and his school. The lines are of irregular length, but bound together by the use of full rhymes and assonances; it is a technique that looks forward to the development of 'free verse' and the modern use of half-rhymes. In his preface to his collected poems Patmore wrote a notable essay on the prosody of English verse, which may have influenced Hopkins in working out his theory of 'sprung verse'. Where Hopkins emphasized the part played by stress in English verse, Patmore showed the relation of rhythm to time: lines of apparently irregular lengths in fact represent time-units of equal duration when the silent pauses that occur within, and at the end of, a line is taken into account. It has been said that Patmore's *Essay on English Prosody* and Hopkins' *Preface* to his own poems contain almost all that has been written on the subject that is of any value whatever.

From THE ANGEL IN THE HOUSE

The 'plot' of *The Angel in the House*, from which the above extracts are taken, is straightforward to the point of banality, and resembles that of a Victorian novelette: in fact it has been suggested that one of Patmore's objects was to show how this kind of story could be used to exhibit the fundamental elements of domestic love. The narrator, Felix Vaughan, belongs to the landed gentry. He returns to Sarum after some years abroad and falls in love with Honoria, the eldest of Dean Churchill's three daughters; he courts her, is accepted, and they get married. The poem relates the growth of their love; describes a ball; recounts their love-letters, Felix's half-hearted ambitions for a political career; there are no extravagant incidents, and it ends with their wedding and honeymoon.

73. *The Cathedral Close*

ll.34–36. Within her face: See George Wither's line in *The Faire Virtue or The Mistress of Philarete* (1622) which has been suggested as a possible model for Patmore's poem.

> If you truly note her face
> You shall find it hath a grace
> Neither wanton, nor o'er serious,
> Not too yielding, nor imperious . . .
> Lowliness hath in her look
> Equal place with greatness took.

76. *Honoria*

l.5. Frederick Graham: Honoria's unsuccessful suitor. He marries on the rebound; and the difficulties of this marriage are the theme of *The Victories of Love*, which forms the sequel to *The Angel in the House*.

79. *Sahara*

l.26. Link catching link: Hopkins criticized this line in one of his letters to Patmore: '"Link catching link": only goods trains do this; passenger trains are locked rigidly.' This is typical of Hopkins' minutely detailed examination of Patmore's poem.

82. *The Prologue*

l.37. Briggs, Factotum, Footman, Butler, Groom: The introduction of 'Briggs'

and the enumeration of his humdrum jobs is a good example of Patm
lightness of touch and his daring and admirable use of the banal to brir
poem down to earth.

84. *The Kites*

The first kite, symbolizing Platonic or purely spiritual love, fails 'for want
of tail'; the second, symbolizing purely sensual love (the poems of Anacreon
celebrate wine, women, and song) is too heavily weighted to fly; the third
kite, 'Vaughan' (the name of the hero of the poem) symbolizes Patmore's
own solution, which combines the idealism of Plato with the earthiness of
Anacreon.

86. *Husband and Wife*

*ll.*1–4. Another example of the skill with which Patmore introduces the
apparently bathetic. The incident of buying the sand-shoes actually happened
to Coventry and Emily Patmore; it was not invented for the poem. This
trivial, apparently fatuous incident serves several purposes: firstly, to show
the whole of married life it is necessary to include the fatuities that are part
of it, but which are transformed by love and given dignity; secondly, the
buying of the sand-shoes symbolizes the responsibilities the bridegroom has
undertaken.

90. AURAS OF DELIGHT

Note the affinity of the theme of this poem with Wordsworth's *Intimations
of Immortality*, which it echoes in places.
*l.*21. *dilaceration:* tearing in pieces.

DANTE GABRIEL ROSSETTI

LIFE

Dante Gabriel Rossetti was born in London in 1828, the eldest son of
Gabriele Pasquale Rossetti, Professor of Italian at King's College, a would-be
poet and political exile from the Kingdom of Naples. His mother was half-
English and a sister of Byron's travelling-companion, Dr Polidori. Rossetti's

family, which included two sisters (Christina, the poet, was the younger) and his brother William, was not well-off, and their poverty increased as the elder Rossetti's health declined. It was no ordinary Victorian household. A stream of exotic political refugees came almost nightly to visit the father and hold endless discussions on Dante and the unification of Italy. Meanwhile Rossetti began his education at King's College School, but left it at the age of 13 to study art. However, he did not care for the teaching at the Royal Academy Schools, and as a result attached himself to Ford Madox Brown, then a little-known artist, as pupil and disciple. About this time he met the young painter William Holman Hunt; the two of them agreed to share a studio. Through Hunt Rossetti met John Everett Millais, the painter, and the sculptor Thomas Woolner. These young artists, with Rossetti's staid and responsible brother William acting as secretary, formed the nucleus of the famous Pre-Raphaelite Brotherhood which came into being in the summer of 1848 when Rossetti was twenty.

The Brotherhood brought valuable publicity to its members when *The Times* attacked a P.R.B. exhibition; upon which John Ruskin, the most influential critic of the day, emerged as its champion. Eventually Ruskin became one of Rossetti's principal patrons. In 1857 Rossetti was commissioned to paint the famous Arthurian frescoes (now practically obliterated) on the ceiling of the new debating hall of the Oxford Union. He enrolled two young men at Oxford, William Morris and Edward Burne-Jones, to help him with the job; they fell completely under his spell, as did Swinburne, who was also at the University. Later Rossetti and Burne-Jones became partners in a firm founded by Morris (who provided the capital) for the production of aesthetic furniture, designs for wallpaper, fabrics, and so on. It was about this time—1860—Rossetti married the enigmatic Elizabeth Siddall ('Guggums', 'The Sid') the archetype of the Pre-Raphaelite ideal of feminine beauty, and model for so many of his paintings, as well as Millais' *Death of Ophelia*. This marriage took place after a ten years' engagement; it was brief and disastrous. By the time he married her Rossetti had fallen in love with Jane Burden, another Pre-Raphaelite beauty who became the wife of William Morris. Meanwhile Elizabeth Siddall had become a neurotic invalid, addicted to laudanum and brandy. In 1862 she died of an overdose of the drug; it is likely she committed suicide. Half out of his mind with remorse, Rossetti buried the manuscripts of his unpublished poems in her coffin.

After her death he took a house in Cheyne Walk which at first he shared with his brother William, Swinburne, and the novelist George Meredith—who soon left, finding the bohemian habits of Swinburne and Rossetti more than he could bear. Swinburne had a habit of sliding naked down the banisters whenever he got drunk, while Rossetti filled the house with a vast menagerie of pets, including a wombat, a zebu, an armadillo a peacock, a kangaroo, and a racoon; he even considered keeping an elephant and training it to clean the windows. Later Rossetti installed one of his models, Fanny Cornforth, as his housekeeper. She proved an expensive acquisition, as it was partly owing to her extravagance that he was harassed by money troubles for the rest of his life.

In 1867 Rossetti began to be afflicted by insomnia, which led to his taking chloral (a drug whose dangerous properties were not then understood). It was at this time he was persuaded to exhume the manuscripts of his poems from his wife's grave. The result of this macabre transaction was the appearance in 1870 of his first volume of poems. Though they won Rossetti fresh fame, their publication inspired an absurd but vicious attack by a Scottish poetaster, Robert Buchanan, who wrote an article called *The Fleshly School of Poetry* indicting them of eroticism, the most deadly sin in Victorian eyes. By then Rossetti was in bad health and in a poor nervous condition. The article had a disastrous effect upon him, made worse by the fact that Rossetti himself shared the prevailing Victorian prudishness. (He once wrote a letter to Tennyson disassociating himself from Swinburne's more libidinous poems.) It led to a breakdown during which he nearly killed himself with a huge dose of the same drug his wife had taken ten years before. But he recovered and for some time was looked after by Jane Morris at Kelmscott Manor. Morris, who had progressive ideas, seems to have been a complaisant husband and used to absent himself in Iceland for the greater part of Rossetti's sojourns at Kelmscott. But his health continued to worsen, and he eventually returned to Cheyne Walk, a victim of persecution mania and hallucinations. These were probably intensified by the chloral with which he dosed himself. For the rest of his life Rossetti was a comparative recluse, though by no means the mental and moral wreck that some of his biographers have depicted. In 1881 his second volume of poems, *Ballads and Sonnets*, was published. He died at Birchington in 1882 at the age of fifty-four.

POETRY

Rossetti was as much a painter as a poet and exhibited similar qualities and weaknesses in either role. On one hand we have a fidelity to detail producing sharpness of imagery; on the other a tendency to the lushly decorative, the fancifully medieval—'a queer and quaint sort of medievalism that was realistic always as long as it could be picturesque' as Ford Madox Ford defined it. In contrast to costume-pieces like *The Blessed Damozel* with their affectations of archaic diction and euphonious furniture of lilies, aureoles, citherns, and

five handmaidens whose names
Are five sweet symphonies,
Cecily, Gertrude, Magdalen,
Margaret and Rosalys

Rossetti could produce austere, almost photographically realized vignettes like *My Sister's Sleep, The Woodspurge,* or *Even So,* where a mood or state of feeling is not so much formulated as transmitted with the utmost precision. Unfortunately this is a vein that Rossetti seldom worked, though it produced almost all his poems that have value. The best of these are represented in this selection.

Apart from *The House of Life* (which is discussed in the introduction) Rossetti's best-known poems are his imitation ballads, of which *Sister Helen* is probably the most successful. But the tagged-on refrains are irritating, though in the case of *Sister Helen* not entirely ornamental. It is in such quasi-medieval poems that Rossetti's debt to Keats is clearest.

Like Poe's, Rossetti's imagination inhabits a vague dream-world; much of his poetry is the poetry of day-dream. This is seen at its best in such pieces as *Love's Nocturn*:

> Valleys full of plaintive air;
> There breath perfumes; there in rings
> Whirl the foam-bewildered springs;
> Siren there
> Winds her dizzy hair and sings.

Such poetry obtains its effects by suggestion, and by a sort of counterpoint between a vague symbology interspersed with precise images, as in these lines:

> Suddenly her face is there:
> So do mounting vapours wreathe
> Subtle-scented transports where
> The black firwood sets its teeth.

In this poem Rossetti looks to some half-defined ideal love to save him from, as it were, the pollution of reality. It is one of his earlier poems and points the way to the later, fragmentary *The Orchard-Pit*, where the ideal love of the first poem has become transformed into a nightmare Life-in-Death like the Spectre-Woman in Coleridge's *Ancient Mariner,* a succubus luring voyagers to their doom. As a poem *The Orchard-Pit* is one of Rossetti's most powerful pieces; as an exploration of the subconscious it may be pertinent epitaph for one who has been described as 'a man without any principles at all, who earnestly desired to find salvation along the lines of least resistance.'

Though so much of his poetry is disappointing to a modern reader, Rossetti is not a negligible poet; and it should not be forgotten that he exercised a decisive influence on the poetry of his time by means of his dynamic personality and flair for discovering talent and even genius in the work of others. It was Rossetti who championed the then almost unknown poetry of Blake and the neglected Keats; who discovered Fitzgerald's *Rubáiyat of Omar Khayyám*; who recognized and encouraged the talent of almost every contemporary poet who had anything of value to offer—apart from such obvious examples as Morris and Swinburne, one could instance lesser-known figures like Ebenezer Jones, who died young, and R. W. Dixon, a still underestimated poet, now best remembered for his friendship and correspondence with G. M. Hopkins.

Notes on the Poems of Dante Gabriel Rossetti

93. MY SISTER'S SLEEP

This is one of the earliest of Rossetti's poems, probably written in his teens; it appeared in the P.R.B. magazine, *The Germ*. The metre is the same as Tennyson's *In Memoriam*, but Rossetti composed his poem some years before Tennyson's was published.

95. LOVESIGHT

This sonnet and the next, and the three lyrics that follow, are taken from *The House of Life*.

98. THE HONEYSUCKLE

Written before his marriage to Elizabeth Siddal. Rossetti had been discussing the moral justification of free love with a friend, and this poem is a symbological allusion to it.

99. THE MIRROR

l. 1. She knew it not: i.e. that the speaker was in love with her. In the next stanza Rossetti compares his situation *vis-à-vis* the woman he loves (but who is unaware of his love) with a man looking at a crowd of people reflected in a mirror; supposing one of them to be himself, he makes a movement, but when the reflected figure makes no similar movement knows he must look elsewhere for his own reflected image. It is a brilliant conceit.

100. THE ORCHARD-PIT

Of this poem Rossetti's brother William noted: 'This is all I can find written of a poem which was long and seriously thought of.' There is in existence Rossetti's prose argument of the poem, a story of a nightmarish Siren who dwelt in a grove of apple-trees and lured men to their doom.

CHRISTINA ROSSETTI

LIFE

Christina Rossetti, the younger sister of Dante Gabriel Rossetti, was born in London on 5th December 1830. Her life was quiet and uneventful. She was educated at home by her mother, and for a time helped to teach at a small day school started by Mrs Rossetti, first in London and afterwards in Somerset. These ventures were made necessary by her father's growing blindness, which had forced him to resign his Professorship at King's College. However, Christina's brother William, a civil servant in the Inland Revenue office, was able to support his mother and sister from 1854 onward. In later life the sales of her poems brought in a small but reasonable income; but she was wholly dependent upon the charity of William till she was nearly forty.

Like her mother, Christina was a strong High Anglican and a devout, even an excessively devout, churchwoman. One of the original members of the Pre-Raphaelite Brotherhood, a somnolent little painter nicknamed 'The Dormouse' for his habit of falling asleep at odd moments, fell in love with Christina, then a girl of great beauty. His name was James Collinson. He had recently become a Roman Catholic; and when he proposed she refused him for that reason. He then reverted to Anglicanism and was accepted. But his conversion did not last; he again became a Roman Catholic, and Christina, understandably put off by this vacillation, broke the engagement. This affair caused her much suffering—she is said to have fainted when she accidentally saw Collinson in the street afterwards—and left its mark on her poetry.

Christina's first poem was published in the *Athenaeum* when she was eighteen, and a year later several more came out in the Pre-Raphaelite magazine, *The Germ*. In 1862 she published her first collection, *Goblin Market and other poems*, which won high praise and was followed in 1866 by *The Prince's Progress*. Her second unhappy love affair took place about this time. In 1860 she became friends with Charles Bagot Cayley, an absent-minded, gentle and retiring scholar, who eventually proposed. But religion was again an obstacle; Cayley was an agnostic, so Christina turned him down—without, however, severing their friendship, which continued till Cayley's death in 1883.

Christina's health was always delicate, and about 1871 she was afflicted by the onset of ophthalmic goitre, a malady that disfigured her for a number of years. She did not mix with society but was not a recluse, being on friendly terms with most of the Pre-Raphaelites, as well as with Coventry Patmore, Swinburne, Browning, and Lewis Carroll. On her brother William's marriage in 1874 she and her mother moved to a house in Torrington Square where she lived for the rest of her life. As she grew older her pietism led her to more and more severe self-deprivations; she gave up going to the theatre, and even playing chess; in her last years she would pick up pieces of paper in the street in case the name of God had been written or printed on them and might be trodden underfoot. She died of cancer in 1894 while in the act of prayer, having outlived all her family except her brother William.

POETRY

Like so many of the Victorian poets Christina Rossetti left behind her a large body of work of uneven value. Her religiosity led her to write a great deal of devotional verse for fasts and saints' days, most of which is not without merit but of not much interest as poetry. Her finest work is to be found almost entirely in the two volumes she published in 1862 and 1866. The first, *Goblin Market and other poems*, is remarkable for the long poem which gives the book its title; it is not undeservedly the best-known of her poems. It has a vitality and sensuousness allied to simplicity, clearness, and intellectual coherence, in notable contrast to the lushness of most poetry of the period. Yet *Goblin Market* has been dismissed as a poem for children, though its underlying theme is serious enough. The younger of two sisters yields to the temptation of tasting forbidden fruit, the wares of the Goblin-men who may be taken to represent the powers of evil purveying sensual delights. Once having tasted the fruit she craves for more, but no second taste is ever given (as John Heath-Stubbs has pointed out, this is a most accurate description of the nature of sensuous sin). She begins to languish and die; but the other sister saves her by attempting to buy the fruit from the goblins while refusing to taste of it herself. They press the fruit against her mouth in the effort to make her do so, and in this way she is able to bring back some of the juices to her sister, who tastes them and recovers. As Heath-Stubbs remarks, 'the point to note is that the central Christian doctrines of guilt, self-sacrifice, and substitution inform the whole poem, giving significance to what seems at first sight no more than a dream-fantasy or a pastiche of a folk-tale.' A more laboured allegory lies behind *The Prince's Progress*, the title-poem of her second book. Here a dilatory Prince (who may typify Everyman) sets out to claim the bride who is waiting for him at the other end of the world, but delays so long on the journey (which includes the crossing of a desert: this is powerfully imagined and the most remarkable part of the poem) that he arrives to find her dead—'Too late for love, too late for joy.'

The most striking thing about these two poems is the peculiar vividness of the imagery—an exactness that is a characteristic Pre-Raphaelite trait. The effect is sometimes that of a Hieronymus Bosch painting. These two poems in themselves express the central themes of Christina's poetry—the conflict felt by a sensuous yet scrupulous nature between delight in the world and the senses, and the necessity for their renunciation; and the loss and frustration she felt after her rejection of marriage. Though Christina's imagination is essentially melancholy, it is not, as some people consider, morbid. She never lost touch with reality, as the other Pre-Raphaelite poets were apt to do. She is at her best in her shorter pieces, some of which achieve a clarity and compression reminiscent of seventeenth-century poets like George Herbert; and they are distinguished by a spare diction untypical of other Victorian poetry. The well-known anthology-piece called *Uphill* is an example; but I have preferred to represent this side of Christina Rossetti's poetry with less familiar but equally fine poems: *The Three Enemies* and *Memory*.

Christina Rossetti is not always given credit for one of her best gifts—she had a remarkably fine ear. This can most easily be appreciated in the lilting gaiety of *Maiden-Song*, but is more subtly evidenced in *Eve*—a poem written, like *Goblin Market*, in a sort of rhymed free verse reminiscent of the medieval poet John Skelton, though without his masculine harshness. Another quality she possesses is wit: and this, together with her psychological insight and gentle sense of humour, enabled her to write delightful pieces like *The Queen of Hearts* and *A Sketch*.

NOTES ON THE POEMS OF CHRISTINA ROSSETTI

IOI. GOBLIN MARKET

The publication of this poem in 1862 achieved the earliest popular success for Pre-Raphaelite poetry. (Swinburne used to call Christina 'the Jael who led our host into victory'.) The irregularity of its metre upset Ruskin, who could not appreciate the subtlety with which Christina handled it; but George Saintsbury, in his *History of English Prosody*, gave it high praise as a display of prosodic skill, pointing out how its 'dedoggerilised Skeltonics' achieve their effect by the skilful grouping of the variations and irregularities that so displeased Ruskin.

In *Goblin Market* the tension between Christina's sensuousness and delight in the visible world, and her distrust of this side of her nature, is vividly expressed. Laura, who yields to the temptation to taste the goblin-fruit, represents the sensuous side of Christina's nature; Lizzie (drawn from

Christina's sister Maria, who was intensely devout and became an Anglican nun) its austere scrupulosity.

l.22. bullaces: wild plums.

l.41. Picking up her golden head: Note the ironical contrast between Lizzie's words and actions.

ll.76–77. wombat, ratel: A wombat is a small Australian marsupial, a ratel is a South African honey-badger. They were among the animals that Christina's brother Dante Gabriel Rossetti kept as household pets at Cheyne Walk.

l.258. succous: juicy.

118. THE THREE ENEMIES

This dialogue between a soul resisting the temptations of the Flesh, the World, and the Devil, is remarkably reminiscent of the devotional poems of George Herbert (1593–1633). See also the poem below, *Memory.*

120. *From* THE PRINCE'S PROGRESS

After his long dilatory journey from the other end of the world the Prince arrives to claim his bride and finds her dead. The poem closes with this dirge sung by the bridesmaids. William Rossetti notes that the stanzas printed here formed the original nucleus of the poem. They were written in 1861 and given the title *The Prince who arrived too late;* at the suggestion of Dante Gabriel Rossetti Christina expanded them into a long narrative poem, *The Prince's Progress,* which became the title-poem of her second collection in 1866.

124. EVE

l.56. conies: rock-rabbits.

ALGERNON CHARLES SWINBURNE

LIFE

Algernon Charles Swinburne was born in London, the eldest son of Admiral Swinburne, on the 5th April 1837. His mother was a daughter of the Earl of Ashburnham, while his father's family had for generations been landed gentry in Northumberland. Swinburne was educated at Eton, and in

1856 entered Balliol College, Oxford. At first he connected himself with John Nichol and a set of republican free-thinkers. But in 1857 he became friends with the second wave of the Pre-Raphaelites—William Morris and Edward Burne-Jones, who had become disciples of Dante Gabriel Rossetti, then painting the frescoes on the ceiling of the Oxford Union. Twice Swinburne attempted and twice failed to win the Newdigate Prize for a poem. Disgusted, he left (or was asked to leave) Oxford in 1860 without having taken a degree.

Swinburne's appearance was as extraordinary as his behaviour. He had a tiny, frail body, electrically fluttering hands; a finely-modelled, dead-white, green-eyed and all but chinless face haloed by a burning fuzz of red hair. To vitality, charm, and an amazing memory was added a highly excitable temperament; it needed very little to set him off into paroxysms of furious screaming. He reacted to impressions with so great an intensity that it blurred for him the line dividing pleasure and pain. This may partly account for his sado-masochistic tendencies, which were to find expression in his poetry as well as in such works as *The Flogging Block*, *The Whippingham Papers*, and *Lesbia Brandon*.

In 1861 he was taken up by Richard Monckton Milnes (by then Lord Houghton) the biographer of Keats and befriender of so many Victorian poets. Lord Houghton introduced him to the works of the Marquis de Sade, in which Swinburne was delighted to find a philosophical justification for his own propensities.

After leaving Oxford Swinburne lived for some time with Rossetti in his ménage—part Bohemian doss-house, part zoo—in Cheyne Walk. About this time he fell in love with Jane Faulkner. He proposed marriage. Greatly startled, the girl burst out laughing. Swinburne, furious and bitterly hurt, thenceforth abandoned all hope of marrying.

Meanwhile, in 1862, he had come upon Baudelaire's *Fleurs du Mal*, which had been banned in France on its first appearance. He wrote an appreciative essay about it for the *Spectator*—an essay in which Gautier's theory of 'l'art pour l'art' (Art for Art's sake) was introduced to English readers. All this time Swinburne had been writing vast quantities of poetry. But his first book (consisting of two verse plays) fell completely flat when it appeared in 1860. However he began writing *Atalanta in Calydon*. It was published in 1865: whereupon Swinburne, like Byron before him, found himself famous overnight. *Poems and Ballads* followed in 1866. But the eroticism of some of the pieces in this book was too much for Victorian decorum, and John Morley wrote a crushing article for *The Saturday Review*, wherein Swinburne found himself labelled as 'the libidinous laureate of a pack of satyrs'. Other reviewers followed Morley's lead, and Swinburne's terrified publisher withdrew the volume, much to the poet's fury. Another publisher was found to reissue the book, and it was not, after all, prosecuted by the police.

176

In 1867 Swinburne met Mazzini, the exiled Italian revolutionary who had dedicated himself to the unification of Italy under a republic. Swinburne, a compulsive hero-worshipper (among his heroes had been Landor, Rossetti, and Victor Hugo) abandoned himself to the domination of Mazzini's personality and devoted himself to writing libertarian and propagandist poems for the cause. They were published in 1871 under the title of *Songs before Sunrise*. But their appearance was belated: by then Italy had been united, though under a monarchy. Mazzini died the following year, leaving Swinburne rudderless.

From thenceforward Swinburne became more and more of a problem to his family and friends. Disastrous forays to London where he made himself ill with drinking and insolvent with debt were interspersed with short recuperative sojourns in the country. At this point Theodore Watts-Dunton, a solicitor and literary aspirant, came on the scene. To begin with he straightened out Swinburne's chaotic business affairs; gradually, by dint of exercising an infinite tact and an inflexible will, he took Swinburne over body and soul. In 1879 he abducted the dying and unresisting poet from his Bloomsbury lodgings and carried him off to a suburban house in Putney where for the next thirty years Swinburne lived on in a sort of posthumous existence, industriously writing and ever more comfortably and hermetically sealed from the world of men, until death came to him in 1909.

POETRY

Swinburne's contemporaries were bowled over by the undeniable metrical virtuosity of his poetry. And it is true that his verse brought a new music to English poetry, even if it now seems rather a barrel-organ music, mellifluous and mechanical. Swinburne was a master of metrical technique, but his ear for the subtler modifications of rhythm cannot compare, for example, with Christina Rossetti's. He was first and last a literary poet. His language came from books, not life. Even the experience on which his poetry draws seems secondhand, except when he is describing the sea, for which his feeling was obsessional. His wide reading in Elizabethan and Jacobean plays, his astonishing scholarship in classical literature, especially Greek, was the nourishment on which he fed his verse. During his long working lifetime he published an enormous quantity of poetry—epics like *Tristram of Lyonesse*, an interminable cycle of plays about Mary Stuart, and any number of odes, sonnets, lyrics, roundels. Most of it is repetitive in effect and may safely be left unread, especially that written in the last thirty years of his life when he was living as Watts-Dunton's prisoner at Putney.

The best of Swinburne's poetry is to be found in his imitation of Greek classical drama, *Atalanta in Calydon*, and in *Poems and Ballads* (first and second series). The glitter and panache of the galloping choruses of *Atalanta* can still be enjoyed. The blank verse is over-adjectivised, though its rhythm has a crispness that is a welcome change from the autumnal languor of Tennyson's. The theme of *Atalanta* is the meaningless cruelty with which the world is governed, and the story revolves round three characters: Althaea the queen of Calydon, her son Meleager, and Atalanta, his beloved. Meleager kills the two brothers of Althaea when they try to seize the hide of the Calydonian boar slain by the huntress Atalanta. Hearing this news, his mother Althaea burns the magic brand on which his life depends; and as it burns away, Meleager dies. As Humphrey Hare has pointed out, 'the main personages are symbols representing the forces of nature as he (Swinburne) saw them in his Sadic pessimism: Althaea, the earth-mother, fecund and fatal; Atalanta, love, the origin of pleasure and pain; and Meleager, suffering humanity, the helpless victim, accepting his destiny with passive fatalism'.

In the *Poems and Ballads* we have rambling lyrical odes, ballads, and elegies in a great variety of metres: *The Leper, A Forsaken Garden, Ave Atque Vale* (the last being an elegy on the death of Baudelaire). Usually they go on far too long, though as T. S. Eliot says of one of them, 'that so little material as appears to be employed in *The Triumph of Time* should realize such an amazing number of words, requires what there is no reason to call anything but genius. You could not condense *The Triumph of Time*. You could only leave out. And this would destroy the poem; though no one stanza seems essential'. In *Dolores, Laus Veneris*, and the *Hymn to Proserpine*, Swinburne startled the Victorians by panegyrizing the sado-masochistic element in sexual love, and by his repudiation of God. But in spite or more probably because of the attacks on them by people like John Morley, they were enthusiastically received by undergraduates of Oxford and Cambridge, who were understandably in revolt against mid-Victorian stuffiness. To them the combination of Swinburne's heady, hypnotic rhythms and shockingness must have been irresistible. Yet Swinburne's poetry was not really a revolt against Victorian sexual morality; rather, it was the obverse of the coin. In Swinburne there is a good deal of the Fat Boy in Pickwick—'I wants to make your flesh creep.' Nonetheless, there is a real vein of imaginative poetry in Swinburne that is not to be found in the rodomontade of the set-pieces designed to *épater les bourgeois*. Whenever the form made it necessary for Swinburne to curb his natural verbal exuberance he usually produced a good poem—for instance *A Jacobite's Farewell*, which, like some of Sir Walter Scott's ballads, is a genuine recreation, rather than a pastiche, of a Border ballad. It is exhibited also in the restrained effectiveness of his sparer poems, such as *After Death*, written under the influence of the Pre-Raphaelite William Morris, and perhaps best of all in his translations of the medieval French poet, François Villon; particularly in the case of *The Epitaph in Form of a Ballad*.

CHORUSES FROM ATALANTA IN CALYDON

127. *When the hounds of spring*

The opening chorus of the play: it is addressed to Artemis, the huntress-goddess (called Diana by the Romans).

l.6. Itylus: The son of the Thracian king Tereus, and of Procne. She murdered Itylus for the sake of her sister Philomena. Philomena was turned into a nightingale and her song is supposed to lament the death of Itylus. Procne, whose tongue had been torn out by Tereus, became a swallow.

l.34. Maenad and Bassarid: names for Bacchantes, the frenzied female votaries of Dionysius.

129. *Before the beginning of years*

l.1–4. T. S. Eliot says of these lines: 'This is not merely "music"; it is effective because it appears to be a tremendous statement, like statements made in our dreams; when we wake up we find that the "glass that ran" would do better for time than grief, and that the gift of tears would be as appropriately bestowed by grief as by time.' But this is not quite fair: it can be argued that time does bring tears; and that grief is not lasting (i.e. its sands run out).

130. *Let your hands meet*

The dying Meleager, attended by his father Oeneus and by Atalanta, is brought in by the Chorus.

140. HYMN TO PROSERPINE

Vicisti, Galilaee: 'Thou hast conquered, Galilean'—i.e. Christ. These are supposed to be the last words of Julian the Apostate, the Roman Emperor who tried to revive paganism.

INDEX OF FIRST LINES